What others about this book ...

"Solo business owners don't have time to waste on marketing theory. Jeanna Pool's book gets right to the point, delivering practical, easy-to-follow marketing strategies that really work."
— **C.J. Hayden**, Author of *Get Clients Now!*

"Your small business will attract all the clients you want quickly and easily by applying the strategies and principles found in this book."
— **Bob Bly**, Author of *Become a Recognized Authority in Your Field*

"A great book on marketing a small business for those entrepreneurs who don't want a lot of fluff or B.S. It's right on the money."
— **Dan S. Kennedy**, Author of *No B.S. Marketing to The Affluent*, www.NoBSBooks.com

"Jam-packed with time-tested strategies that really work. Apply them to your small business marketing and profit!"
— **Jay Conrad Levinson**, Author of the bestselling Guerilla Marketing series of books

"This book is a great kick in the pants and will jump-start the success of marketing your small business."
— **Joe Vitale**, Author of *The Attractor Factor*, www.MrFire.com

"Avoid costly mistakes in your marketing efforts by studying this gem of a marketing resource!"
— **Al Ries,** Co-author of the bestselling book *The Fall of Advertising and the Rise of P.R.*

"If you're comfortable with the technical aspect of your business but feel totally lost when it comes to marketing your business, then congratulations—you've just found the book that's going to show you the way. Jeanna knows her stuff. Invest in this valuable resource and watch your business and your bottom line thrive."

— **Bob Burg,** Author of *Endless Referrals: Network Your Everyday Contacts into Sales*

"This book spells out simple and proven strategies that actually work for small businesses to gain more clients and become much more profitable. In fact, the answer to 'what you do for a living' found in Chapter 5 is worth 10 times this book's price."

— **Yanik Silver,** Internet Marketing Expert and Creator of *Instant Sales Letters*

"A handy, concise and wonderful resource on marketing that will serve your solo small business for years to come."

— **Dr. Ivan Misner,** Founder of BNI-Business Network International and Author of *Masters of Success*

"An indispensable guide to marketing a small business that you'll turn to again and again…grab your highlighter, you'll be marking this one up."

— **John Jantsch,** Author of *Referral Flood* and Founder of *Duct Tape Marketing*

"Jeanna has laid out a solid marketing plan that WORKS. Every small business owner and solo-preneur should own and use this book!"

— **Alexandria Brown,** Online Entrepreneur and Marketing Coach, www.AliBrown.com

Marketing for Solos®

THE Ultimate How-To Guide For Marketing Your One Person Small Business Successfully

Marketing for Solos®

THE Ultimate How-To Guide For Marketing Your One Person Small Business Successfully

Jeanna Pool

3 BAR press • Denver, Colorado

Marketing for Solos®: THE Ultimate How-To Guide For Marketing Your One Person Small Business Successfully, By Jeanna Pool

Originally published under the title: When Your Small Business is YOU™ Marketing Handbook, revised and updated.

Published by: 3 BAR press, P.O. Box 460114, Denver, Colorado 80246

Author's Note: Throughout this book, I have drawn heavily on examples from current and past clients; however, to protect their privacy, names, industries, case studies and details have been purposely altered and disguised and some of the examples and stories used have been fictionalized.

Marketing for Solos® is a registered trademark of Jeanna Pool and CATALYST creative, inc., Denver, Colorado and may not be used without written permission from the author. Visit Jeanna's website: **www.MarketingForSolos.com** for more information, free resources, articles, tips and strategies designed to help you market your solo small business successfully and attract clients consistently.

Warning—Disclaimers
This book is designed to provide information on marketing and promoting a small business. It is sold with the understanding that the publisher and author are not engaged in rendering legal, accounting or other professional services. If legal or other expert assistance is required, the services of a competent professional should be sought. It is not the purpose of this book to reprint all of the information that is otherwise available to small business owners, but instead to complement, amplify and supplement other texts. You are urged to read all the available material, learn as much as possible about marketing and promoting a small business and tailor the information to your individual needs. Marketing is not a get-rich-quick scheme. Anyone who decides to start, run and market and promote a small business must expect to invest a lot of time, effort and money in it. Every effort has been made to make this book as complete and accurate as possible. However, there may be mistakes, both typographical and in content. Therefore, this text should be used only as a general guide and not as the ultimate source of marketing and promoting a small business. Furthermore, this book contains information on marketing and promoting a small business that is current only up to the printing date. The purpose of this book is to educate and to entertain. Throughout this book the author provides links to recommended resources, in some cases the author will receive compensation based on the recommendation. The author or publisher shall have neither liability nor responsibility to any person or entity with respect to any loss or damage caused, or alleged to have been caused, directly or indirectly, by the information, writing, examples, recommendations, links to resources and opinions contained in this book. **If you do not wish to be bound by the above, you may return this book to the publisher for a full refund.**

If you find any typographical errors in this book, they are here for a reason. Some people love looking for them and we strive to please as many people as possible.

ISBN 978-0-9769962-7-9

Printed in the United States of America.
10 9 8 7 6 5 4 3 2 1

Dedicated to all of my current and past clients.

Without you, I would not be where I am today.
Thank you.

Contents

Acknowledgments

There is absolutely no way I could have written this book without the generous help and support from many fantastic people without them, this book simply would not exist.

I wish to extend a huge, heartfelt thank you to *all* of the wonderful solo small business owners who contributed their time, feedback, examples and questions used in the book. There are way too many to mention all by name, but your help has been incredible. Thank you, thank you!

Thank you to all of my current and past clients, whom this book is dedicated to. Because of you, I have never worked a day in my solo small business life. You make everything I do an absolute pleasure!

Thank you to the incredible group of solo small business owners who are members of The Greater Denver Group Chapter of BNI in Denver, Colorado for their business, referrals and friendship.

Thank you to my awesome GKIC Mastermind Group for challenging me to think bigger, supporting me in seeing my vision and goals become a reality, and walking beside me to hear and flesh out all of my crazy, off-the-wall ideas.

I'm very grateful for my wonderful friends and family who make my life a blast: Rhonda, Carrie (a little marketing each day), Mark, Dwayne, Rick, Marilyn, Michele, Leilani, Bev, Laurie, Connie, Sandra, Cindy, the Schuckman clan, Barbara Henderson (the life of any party) and so many others!

Much love and a *huge* thanks to my Mom—the hardest-working and most successful solo small business owner I know—I couldn't have done it without you! For my Dad, who passed away in 1996, I wish he was still here to see the book completed.

I thank my editor, Michael Bremer of UnTechnical Press.

And lastly, a very special thank you to John Eggen of Mission Publishing and the Mission Marketing Mentors Publishing Program. With John's mentoring and teaching, I learned everything I needed to know about writing a book and making it a reality. Thank you!

What Is A Solo?

Sure, this book is titled Marketing for Solos®, but you may be thinking, "What exactly *is* a solo anyway?!?" If so, then let's take a moment to define what a solo truly is …

According to the dictionary the word solo means: Something undertaken or done alone. Of, relating to, or being one person. Done without a companion.

Great definitions, but for the purpose of this book and everything you'll learn inside, the definition of a solo is: a one-woman or one-man small business owner. It's as simple as that.

You can be married, divorced or single. You can be an only child or one of many siblings. You can have a college degree or be a high school dropout. You can have a background in corporate America or have started your business from scratch … bottom line: whatever your family life, private life or past work life looks like, that doesn't matter.

What matters is …

You are your small business and your small business is you. *You* are the business and *you* are the brand. Clients are buying you (I'll talk more about this in the Introduction found on Page 17). You are the main force behind your business. You are the one running the show and calling the shots. You are the one doing the work for your clients, and while you may have an assistant, or a contractor who helps you, you don't have a large staff of employees to manage. You work with clients one-on-one—either face to face or virtually via email or by phone. Your clients can be just around the corner or across the globe. You provide services to your clients, and for the most part, the product you "sell" is your expertise. You may be a life coach, business coach, consultant, author, speaker, trainer, therapist, writer, designer, architect, contractor, attorney, accountant, real estate agent, mortgage broker, travel agent, chiropractor, dentist, massage therapist, photographer, or another type of service based professional. You may have heard yourself referred to as a "solo-prenuer", "solo-professional" or "independend professional."

If any or all of this sounds familiar … then you are a solo … a solo small business owner to be exact. And marketing you as a solo is what this book is all about.

Your FREE Gift
(And we all love free, don't we?!?)

Over **$497** In
Marketing Tools
and Resources
Yours **FREE!**

As a very special thank you for purchasing this book, Jeanna Pool has a gift for you ... a collection of valuable marketing tools, strategies and resources. Together, these normally sell for over $497, but as an owner of this book, they're yours absolutely free! To get your free gift simply visit: www.MarketingForSolos.com/book-gift and follow the instructions.

Welcome To The Family!

Wow, that headline sounds like something that would be said during a Godfather movie, doesn't it? But, truly I want to welcome you to the family and congratulate you on making the very smart decision to purchase this book. Because this book is only the beginning …

Being a solo small business owner is awesome! You probably agree. I wouldn't trade being my own boss for the world. But, as one of my mentors, Bill Glazer says, "Being an entrepreneur can sometimes be the loneliest job in the world." And I would have to agree with him. I think being a small business owner and entreprenuer can be lonely at times, especially as a solo. Our friends and family may not understand why we want to run our own business. When we have successes, they celebrate, but may not completely get it. When we have setbacks or a few failures, they may think we're a bit nuts and ask, "Don't you ever miss a 'real' job with a steady paycheck?"

Well, by reading this book, you are now a part of the family … the Marketing for Solos® family. What I mean by this is, yes, you are a solo, but that doesn't mean you're alone.

The first step is to read this book. By doing so, you're going to be well on your way to generating stellar results from all of your marketing efforts and activities. The next step is to stay plugged in. This will keep you moving forward and motivated long after you finish the last page. So once you've finished the book, here's how to keep moving forward …

➤ Visit www.MarketingForSolos.com. The website contains a wealth of information, tools and resources to help you with the marketing of your solo small business.

➤ While at the website, visit the Free Stuff section. There you can download free information, as well as, sign up for our free eZine that's jam-packed with marketing ideas, techniques and strategies to keep you moving forward and generating results.

➤ Consider enrolling in the Marketing for Solos® Academy. This program gives you personal guidance, mentoring, teaching, resources and accountability to help keep you plugged in and motivated, so you can market your services successfully *and* consistently. More information is at www.MarketingFor SolosAcademy.com

Introduction

(Start here! No really, read this first.)

Will this book really help you market your services better, more easily and more successfully? The answer is YES, if two things are true: One. Your small business is you, meaning, you are selling, well, you: *your* services, *your* expertise, *your* experience, what *you* can do for your clients.

Sure, you may think you sell massage therapy, chiropractic care, real estate, investment advice, interior design, business coaching or whatever else you do. But, in reality, you are selling you. You are your small business. And if that's the case, this is the book for you!

Two. You are a solo, meaning, you are a one-woman or one-man show. You don't have a herd of staff, you don't have a bunch of employees. You are the solo captain of your small business ship and you like it that way. If that's the case, this is the book for you!

I'm not going to teach you theory or jargon or Marketing 101 college textbook examples or how big corporations market themselves and how you can copy them. Nope. I am going to talk about what really works when you're a solo. You see, this book is one-of-a-kind! It's a system that actually works for solo small businesses. Too many marketing books out there don't apply to the one person gif. But, not this book. This book is very different (as you will soon see).

The information is arranged in a step-by-step, logical sequence of things that you need to learn and put into action, one after the other, to ensure that you'll be successful in marketing your services.

You're going to learn a lot. You'll learn how to end marketing struggles. You'll learn what really works and what doesn't. You'll know how to steer clear of costly mistakes. You'll learn how to make marketing manageable and doable. You'll have all the tools and strategies you'll need for your marketing efforts. In fact, by the time you finish this book, you'll know, understand, and have a system (The Marketing for Solos® System) to market your solo small business successfully again and again and again.

If you're struggling with marketing, that struggle ends right here. If you want better results from your marketing, success starts right here. Use what you learn in this book over and over and over again, and you *will* succeed. The system you'll learn, WILL work for your solo small business!

One last thing before we dive in … don't let this book become "shelf help" meaning you read a little, stick it on a shelf and forget about it. You gotta put things into action and actually apply what you learn! When you do, your success will be unlimited.

And, be sure to visit **www.MarketingForSolos.com**. There you will find a wealth of resources, ideas, articles and strategies, plus a ton of free goodies for you … all geared to help you market your services successfully and attract more clients on a consistent basis!

Wishing you MUCH success,
Jeanna Pool

CHAPTER 1

Where You Are and Where You Can Be

Whether you started your own solo small business yesterday, three years ago or over a decade ago, I want you to take a minute and think back. Think back to the time you decided to take the plunge into entrepreneurship … when you decided to start your own business.

No more punching the time clock. No more working for someone you may not have been that fond of. No more working your tail off for a measly two-weeks vacation and a bonus or raise here and there. You decided to be your own boss, set your own hours, and do what you love on your terms.

Do you remember? Boy, I sure do.

Being an only child doesn't really prepare you for a life of "living by the boss's rules." I was never really all that good at working for other people. There finally came a time when I simply had enough. It was time to take the experience, expertise and passion of my craft and face the business world on my own.

How about you? Why did you start you own business? Why did you leave the "comfort" and "security" of a steady paycheck?

If you're like most of us, you started your own small business because you have a love and passion for what you do. If I had to guess, I'd say 99% of all solo small business owners start out this way—a love and passion for what they do, and a desire to set their own hours and be their own boss.

But here's the catch: just because you have a love and a passion and are really good at what you do, doesn't mean you will be able to make a living at it. You still have to market yourself and consistently attract clients, or you won't make it.

We've all heard the scary statistics that many, if not most, small businesses fail in the first few years.

This brings us to some all important questions ...

Why do so many small businesses fail? Why do so many small businesses struggle? Why is it that way too many small business owners—who are absolutely phenomenal at what they do, are experts in their field, can provide their services better than anyone else and are the absolute experts in their industry—struggle to attract enough clients to make ends meet?

I'm sure there are a plethora of reasons—lack of money, the economy taking a nosedive—but, from my perspective, I'd have to say most small businesses struggle, fumble and ultimately fail for one simple reason—lack of clients. And a lack of clients is a result of one thing—a lack of effective marketing.

If your marketing is effective, you will attract clients. If it's not, you won't. It just doesn't get any simpler than that.

When you really think about this, it makes total sense. Again, more than likely, you started your small business because you're really good at what you do or have a huge passion and talent for it. But chances are, you're probably not that good at marketing yourself to attract clients consistently. Sound familiar?

Well, guess what? That can change. You can be very successful at marketing your small business. You can be very successful at standing out from the crowd and attracting clients consistently.

The way to do this is by understanding the proven strategies for marketing your small business as a solo. This is very different from marketing products like computers or running shoes. And, this is very different than marketing your services when you have a ton of staff. You're marketing your services as the one-man or one-woman show, and in doing so, you're marketing 'you' as the small business that can solve your clients' pain, problem or predicament. You're the expert. YOU are the product that people are buying. Never forget that!

When you understand this, when you know the fundamentals, when you know the strategies, when you know what works and what doesn't work, and have a proven system, the world is your oyster.

Ready to jump in and start attracting clients right now? Great! However, there is one more thing I must ask you: Are you willing to do whatever it takes to be successful?

You see, as a solo and when your small business is you, you can't float your way through. You can't just "try" to have your own small business and see what happens. You can't just "try this marketing thing." You must be committed. You must, in your heart and mind do whatever it takes to be successful. That means actually doing the things you will learn in this book. Putting the system you learn into practice. Don't just read; act. And, as I mentioned earlier, don't let this book become "shelf help." Let's dive in. ◆

The Cold, Hard Truth

Before we step into the tools, methods, language and activities you'll use to successfully market your small business, I have some bad news. This may come as a shock to you. For most people, it does. But, if I didn't share it with you, I'd be doing you a huge disservice.

I call it the cold, hard truth. I call it this because it is a little cold and a little hard, but full of truth.

Most solo small business owners have never heard this truth before. Some who have, believe it. Some who have, don't. But the fact remains ... it is, in fact, true.

If you keep this truth in your mind every day you market yourself and every time you speak to a potential client, you will be light-years ahead of your competition. In fact, you'll leave your competition in the dust.

No One Cares

The cold hard truth is … prospects do not care about you. Sorry, they don't. Prospects do not care about your degrees, your years of experience, your years in your industry, how many awards you've won or how great you think you are. Prospects care about one thing and one thing only—themselves.

You see, we human beings are, by nature, well, selfish. Some, of course, more than others, but we are all selfish in some measure simply because we are human. We put ourselves first. We put our family, our property and our valuables first and foremost. It's the same with your prospects. They care about one thing: themselves.

Claude C. Hopkins wrote a book back in the 1920's called *Scientific Advertising*. Here is what he says about prospects caring about themselves versus caring about you:

> "Remember the people you address are selfish, as we all are. They care nothing about your interests or your profit. They seek service for themselves. Ignoring this fact is a common mistake and a costly mistake in advertising. Ads say in effect, "Buy my brand. Give me the trade you give to others. Let me have the money." This is not a popular appeal. The best ads ask no one to buy. That is useless. Often they do not quote a price. The ads are based entirely on service. They offer wanted information." [1]

Pretty powerful and yet written long ago. The same is true today. The cold, hard truth is: prospects do not care about you. They only care about themselves. This isn't because your prospects are evil people, it's simply because they are human.

---

1 Claude C. Hopkins, *Scientific Advertising*, (1886-1932).

Think about it. You and I are exactly the same way. Imagine a telemarketer calling to sell you something. You won't really care that he was the top salesman for last month or that he has been with the company the longest and is the most experienced in sales.

No, you'll only care about one thing: will the product that he is selling benefit me, meet my wants, needs and desires at a fair price? If yes, you buy, if no, you say "not interested" and hang up the phone. You care about you, not about him. That doesn't make you evil, it makes you completely normal.

Ingrain this in your conscious and subconscious. Post this on the mirror in your bathroom and on the computer monitor in your office. Read it everyday.

The Cold, Hard Truth ...
Prospects do not care about you, they only care about themselves.

The Good News
There is some very good news in all of this. You now know the cold, hard truth. Most of the solo small businesses you're competing against for clients don't have a clue about this, so you can use this knowledge to your advantage.

The way to profit from the cold, hard truth is to learn to flip-flop the way you present information about your services to a prospect. Instead of focusing on yourself first, by boasting that you have been in business since 1967, or that you are a Gold Star member of the Better Business Bureau, or that you have offices in Japan, New York and Toronto, or that you have won numerous awards for your work, you have to focus on the prospect first and yourself last.

The way to do this is to focus on the prospects 3 P's: pain, problem or predicament. We are going to spend a lot of time in Chapter 5 working on this skill, but for now you need to accept and understand that this is the first major shift in your marketing that will make a huge difference in your success.

From now on, you must stop talking about yourself first and the prospect last. Always focus on the prospect first and on yourself at the very end. ◆

Key Concept
The Cold Hard Truth: Prospects do not care about you, they only care about themselves. Use this to your advantage in all of the marketing you do, by always focusing on the prospect first and on yourself at the very end.

CHAPTER 3

Change Your Thinking

To successfully market your solo small business over the long haul, you're going to have to change your thinking. In the last chapter, you learned the cold, hard truth that prospects do not care about you, they only care about themselves. In order to be successful, your thinking needs to shift to the way the prospect thinks, and that way of thinking has to guide the way you present your services and market them. Once you start thinking like a prospect, your efforts will be much more successful.

Everything is Backwards

The reason why so many solo small businesses' marketing efforts fail is because they're doing everything backwards. You, more than likely, are doing everything backwards, as well.

You talk about and sell yourself first, when in actuality you should be last. You focus on yourself, so you can prove that you know what you are talking about, when, in actuality, you should focus only on your prospect. You think that prospects care, when in actuality they don't. You put yourself first, saying that you can do this and you can do that ... but the prospect wants to hear about *himself.* Everything you do is backwards, and that is why your marketing efforts fail.

What Needs to Change

Your thinking needs to change in four areas:

1. Who you focus on

Instead of focusing on you, focus on the prospect first. It's no longer all about you—it's now all about the prospect.

2. What you focus on

Instead of speaking about how great and wonderful you are—your qualifications, degrees, awards and expertise—focus on the 3Ps of the prospect—pain, problem or predicament.

3. How you focus

Instead of telling of your great work and process, focus on the language of results and how your service will benefit the prospect.

4. Your marketing mindset

Whether you think marketing is hard or easy ... you're right. If you approach marketing as a chore to drudge through, you will not be successful. You have to change your mindset to the belief that marketing is easy. And it is, once you know what will work and what won't.

Marketing is not hard if you know the fundamentals. It's just like sports. In basketball, you may have a guy who can slam dunk from the free throw line, as many basketball legends can, but unless your team practices the fundamentals of good defense, making free throws and conditioning, the team won't win a lot of games.

In weight lifting, professional body builders don't fool around with all of the fancy-schmancy workout equipment. They utilize the fundamentals of a good set of dumbbells and barbells, bench press, squats, curls, push-ups, pull-ups and the like.

Working the fundamentals will make marketing easier. Now, does that mean that successful marketing won't take a lot of hard work? Absolutely not. You can't slack and expect to get results. You have to take action. You have to work hard, but once you know the fundamentals *and* work at them—just like you would in sports—your marketing will be much easier.

These are major shifts and changes in thinking that many small business owners miss. What's amazing is, once you start thinking this way—focusing on the prospect first, focusing on the prospect's pain, problem or predicament and focusing on results—prospects will be drawn to you. They will sit up and take notice of what you have to offer and think, "Hey, this person really knows me and what I want to accomplish. They really understand." Changing your thinking is how you generate stellar results.

Give to Receive

You've probably heard the saying, "Give to receive." As a kid, I heard my mother and grandmother say this to me and I thought, "Are you crazy? Why in the world would I want to give before I get?" (Did I mention I'm an only child?)

Unfortunately, too many solo small businesses think the same way, even today, as I did as a young kid. "Why should I give before I receive?" Most small business owners approach marketing from a *get* mentality versus a *give* mentality. You've undoubtedly run into them: I need to get clients. I need to get more business. I need to get more money. I need to get _____ (insert your own noun here).

This is the complete opposite of how small business owners should market their services. If you want your marketing efforts to be very successful, give to receive.

Why is Giving So Powerful?

Giving is a fundamental principle in life, and when applied to the marketing of your small business, the results can be phenomenal. Giving follows what's known as the *Universal Law of Reciprocation*, which basically means: when you give something to someone, do something nice for someone or help out someone—expecting nothing in return—they will more times than not feel compelled to give back to you. This is human nature.

Dr. Robert B. Cialdini, Ph.D. in his book *Influence: The Psychology of Persuasion* illustrates this fact by saying:

"Make no mistake, human societies derive a truly significant competitive advantage from the reciprocity rule, and each of us knows about the social sanctions and derision applied to anyone who violates it. The labels we assign to such a person are loaded with negativity—moocher, ingrate, welsher. Because there is general distaste for those who take and make no effort to give in return, we will often go to great lengths to avoid being considered one of their number." [2]

Think about it: when someone does something nice for you, don't you want to do something nice back? When someone sends you a gift, don't you send them a thank you note? Have you ever heard someone say, "I owe him a favor for _____."?

Think of people who have turned you off and others who you were drawn to. Were you turned off because they seemed selfish? Were they pushy? Did they seem to care only about themselves and not about you? Were you drawn to them because they put you first—without expecting anything in return? Did they do you a favor? Help you out with something? Give you valuable free advice? How did that make you feel? Pretty good, probably. Of course, we will always be drawn to those who give first and do things for us without expecting anything in return. Why? The Universal Law of Reciprocation.

The lesson learned here is: when marketing your small business, give first without expecting anything in return.

What to Give

For solo small businesses where you are the business, the absolute best thing to give away is your knowledge and expertise. This runs completely contrary to what most sales experts and even some marketing experts say. They teach that you should never give away your expertise because you'll be giving away what you can be paid for. The key is to balance—give away enough so prospects will see you as

---

2 Dr. Robert B. Cialdini, Ph.D., *Influence: The Psychology of Persuasion* (New York, NY: Quill, William Morrow and Company, Inc., 2003). Pages 19-20.

the absolute expert, but don't give away everything you know. Give enough away to whet their appetite, so they will keep coming back for more. You can do this in several ways:

Free Trials or Demos

Massage therapists do this often and with great success. You'll see them at sporting events or outside the local health food stores, setting up their chair and giving away free ten-minute massages. Why do they do this? To give potential clients a feel—literally—for what they can do and how they can make their clients feel better.

How can you give potential clients a free trial of your services? If you're a business or life coach, how about a free 30-minute or one-hour coaching session, so prospects can get a taste of how you would work together? Maybe you're an interior designer and can do a free demo to show a client the process you use to color coordinate a room for a better feeling of warmth and comfort.

Free Information

Articles, info packages, tip sheets, multi-page reports—all of these are great ways to give something to a prospect while illustrating your expertise. An accountant may develop a booklet entitled *Ten Ways To Cut Your Taxes* and give it to all of his prospects. Not only are you giving away something of value, you're illustrating your expertise at the same time. A prospect who reads this will naturally be drawn to the accountant for giving away great information that can help.

Free Workshops or Talks

Realtors and financial advisors use free workshops or talks very effectively. Again, it shows prospects your expertise in your industry. You are giving away valuable help and information, while demonstrating that you know what you are talking about and that you are the person the prospect should work with.

Free Positive Surprises

Why not just send your past clients or prospects a free surprise, like a gift card, movie tickets or some other little gift? The possibilities are endless, and doing this will really make you stand out from the crowd. I do this with my current and past clients quite a bit. At random times of the year, they get a note and a little goodie from me for no reason at all—just because. When I do this, the Universal Law of Reciprocation never, ever fails to kick in. I always get something back, from a phone call with a heartfelt thank you, to a referral, to another project from a client … I always get something in return.

But, But, But

Now, some of you may be thinking, "Jeanna, this giving thing is great, and I agree; but I need money, I need clients. I gotta get something in return." Don't worry, you will. You will receive. But, if you give off the perception that it is all about you, you, you and you have to *get* something first before you give, you lose. Because you will appear needy and selfish, and no one wants to do business with a needy/selfish small business owner. Right? I don't want to do business with a needy/selfish small business owner, and I bet you agree.

So, trust in the Universal Law of Reciprocation, trust that it will work for you as it works for me and for so many others. Market yourself from a giving state. Give away your knowledge, give away a trial, give away a sample, give away your time, give away whatever it is in your world that will give your prospects value, help, or ideas. This is what will make you shine as the expert and ultimately attract prospects to want to do business with you. ◆

Key Concept

Change Your Thinking and Give to Receive: Up until now everything you were doing for marketing your services is backwards. It's time to change your thinking about who you focus on, what you focus on, how you focus and your marketing mindset. It's also time to embrace the concept of giving to receive. It's no longer all about you, you, you. So ask yourself ... what can you give your prospects that will whet their appetite to learn more about you and your services? What can you give them so they'll want to get to know you better? What can you give them so they'll realize you understand their pain, problem or predicament and therefore naturally be drawn to doing business with you?

Find Your Niche and You'll Get Rich

I t never fails. I can ask ten different solo small business owners who they work with and more times than not, at least eight out of the ten, and usually ten out of ten, will answer, "Anyone who …".

What about you? How would you answer my question? Would you, too, answer "Anyone who …" or "Everyone who …" or how about "Someone who is …"? If you said yes, you're like many other solo small business owners, but you're making a key mistake in identifying your target market—who you work with.

What's Wrong with Anyone, Everyone and Someone?

The problem with saying you work with "anyone, everyone and someone" is that those descriptions really don't tell exactly who it is you work with. They are too generic. They are too broad. And, in essence, you're trying to be all things to all people.

When you say "anyone, everyone and someone," people's minds just shut down. Ask someone at a networking event, "Do you know anyone who …?" Chances are, they're going to say to themselves, "Anyone, hmmm … I don't know 'anyone'." And they'll verbalize, "Nope, sorry. I really don't know anyone who …". They can't think of anyone because 'anyone' is just too vast and too much to wrap their minds around. That's the problem. That's why this is a key mistake.

You must be specific—very specific—in your description of who you work with. Being specific helps people think of others they know who can use your services. Being specific helps prospects see themselves in your description and know that you are the person to work with. In fact, you want to be so specific that people think of a specific person—by name. You want them to say, "Ah, Julie, yeah, Julie needs this. You have to call Julie!" Or, "You know I really need help with that. Can we talk further?"

Let me give you an example from a small business owner I know. A nutritionist who focuses on natural health and herbal supplements was struggling to get referrals. The big problem was that he, like most other small business owners, was in the "anyone, everyone and some-one" modus operandi.

One very specific area of his business is, he offers a natural, herbal supplement that helps people completely eliminate jet lag when they travel. Eventually he started to focus on this specific area of his business when he talked to prospects and those who could refer clients to him.

It worked like magic. He got many referrals from people who were traveling overseas and wanted to avoid jet lag. Because he was specific, prospects could wrap their minds around what he offered and would think, "Hey I need this!" and, just like that, he'd get a new client.

When you talk in specifics, people think in specifics. People know who and how to refer you. Prospects see themselves in your description, and you get more business. The great thing is, as in the case of the nutritionist, eliminating jet lag was just one, small aspect of how he helps his clients. He can build on that success by focusing on a few very detailed descriptions of who he works with. The results will be very effective.

The same thing will happen with your small business, once you eliminate "anyone, everyone and someone" and start being specific about who you work with.

Find a Niche and You'll Get Rich

Find a niche and you'll get rich. Have you ever heard that saying? I don't know who said it or where I was the first time I heard it, but, oh, my, is it ever true! I'd like to add to the "find a niche and you'll get rich" mantra. I think it should really be "find a niche, specialize in that niche, constantly market to that niche and become known as 'the specialist', the 'absolute authority' and the 'guru' in that niche and you'll get very, very rich."

I like to call this "hit them right between the eyes and knock 'em dead." Because when you find a niche and become a specialist in that niche, wow, you will knock your prospects socks off—not to mention knocking them out and knocking the cover off of the ball in your marketing.

Why is Finding a Niche and Specializing in That Niche So Important?

There are a few things you need to realize about people ... the same people who are your prospects ... the same people you have been telling you work with "anyone, everyone and someone."

First and Foremost ...

People want to work with specialists, not generalists. When you try to market to anyone, everyone and someone, what ends up happening is that you become a jack-of-all-trades and a master of none. You can't be all things to all people.

"Anyone, everyone and someone" are very general and very generic terms. Everyone likes a specialist—they are sought after. Not as many like to work with generalists—people don't usually seek them out.

Do you want better clients? Do you want more money? Do you want your marketing to be much, much easier? Then you have to stop being a generalist and specialize in a niche.

I want you to imagine for a moment that you had some kind of rare disease—a life-and-death situation. Would you go to your general practice family doctor for treatment, or would you seek out the absolute best medical specialist in the world? Of course, the answer is you'd seek out the specialist. The same can happen for you, if you will find a niche and specialize in it. People will seek you out, travel long distances and make special effort to work with you—just like you'd do for the specialist who can help you with your rare disease, even if he was located half way around the world.

I know a massage therapist whose niche is pregnant women—a large part of her client base is pregnant women—and she does very well in this niche. She's referred to again and again. She has become known as *the* massage therapist to go to when the pain, aches, sleepless nights and sometimes agony of being pregnant is too much. It's easy to refer business to her ... because she essentially, is a specialist, in this niche.

Second ...

If you find a niche and specialize in that niche, you'll create a name for yourself, just like the specialist who's the expert in your rare disease. You will become known in the field for your specialty. Colleagues in your industry will refer prospects to you. Just think, a competitor in your industry saying this to a prospect of yours, "Oh, you have that rare disease, well go see Dr. John Doe at The XYZ Medical Institute; he's the specialist and expert in that rare disease. Here's his number; you should call him today." It can and will happen. I see it everyday. The same can happen to you, but you must find a niche and specialize.

Third ...

You will be able to charge higher fees and make more money if you find a niche and specialize. This is true in a lot of industries, especially medicine. Specialists in the field of medicine make a lot more money than their general practice colleagues. I can guarantee you that the specialist you went to see for your rare disease cost you much more than the family doctor you have gone to since you were four years old. Specialists in the field of medicine charge two, three, four and more times as much as general practice doctors. And you know what ... people pay it all the time—you would, wouldn't you? I mean this person is *the* specialist. You have a rare disease and he is the best in the world to help. You'd pay the high fee, just like thousands of others would.

Why? Because he is the specialist. He is the best. He knows what he is doing in this specific area, so he is worth the extra money that you are willing to pay. And, as an added bonus to being a specialist in a particular niche, most of the time, specialists in a particular niche are not questioned about their price or haggled with for a discount. Sometimes you will hear a grumble such as, "Man, that doctor is expensive!" But almost immediately after the grumble, someone else will say, "Yeah, but he's the specialist and expert in that field, so he's worth it." The same can happen for your solo small business.

Fourth ...

You will attract bigger and better clients by finding a niche and specializing in it. People will be easier to work with, because they want to work with you—the specialist, the name in the field, the one to hire, the absolute best choice. They won't dig and prod and beg and pressure for a discount. They will be more fun to work with because they actually want to work with you. They want the best, they expect the best, they have sought out the best—you, the specialist—and so they will love working with you, and you'll most likely love working with them.

Fifth ...

You will get really, really, really, really good at your specialty and at the service you provide for your clients. Think about it: you will be specializing in a particular area and therefore do and see this area time and time and time again. You will be able to quickly and easily solve problems. Your clients will think you're a genius. And while you may well be one, it's simply that you're the expert in a particular area and thus spend your days working, fixing, solving and servicing problems, issues and situations in that area, and that adds to your expertise for your clients. Coming up with a solution—a very good and successful solution—will be 100 times easier for you than for anyone else.

Have I convinced you that finding a niche and specializing in that niche is a surefire way to make the marketing for your solo small business a success?

Before we get into the nitty-gritty of how to find a niche, I want to address a question that I know is gnawing at some of you right now. I hear you saying, "But Jeanna, if I find a niche and become a specialist in that niche, I am going to get really bored focusing all of my time and energy and effort on one niche, one industry, one type of client. I think I'd rather have a root canal with a butter knife!"

I hear exactly what you're saying—I get this comment all the time. But, I *never* said that this is the *only* thing you have to focus your time and energy on.

It is imperative to focus on a niche. But, you can take on any other clients you feel would be a good fit to add variety and spice to your business. You can have as many different clients in as many different industries as you want. Of course, you're doing the whole "anyone, everyone and someone" thing again, but, what I am saying is that to successfully market your business, you need to find at least one niche, one area, or one industry to specialize in.

It is imperative to do this because of all of the reasons I just listed above. But, you can take on any other clients you feel would be a good fit to add variety and spice in your business.

Once you have dominated one niche and have attracted a full client load, you can find another niche to be involved in, and so on. I know several small business owners who focus on and dominate four, five, and even more different niches.

Don't be surprised, though, if you find yourself staying with your niche. Many solo small business owners who have found a niche, specialized in that niche and gone on to become the expert in that niche have shifted their entire business to focus solely and completely on that niche. I mean ... rolling in the vast piles of money is a very hard thing to argue with.

How to Find a Niche

There are two main ways to find a niche and become the specialist in that niche. The first is to just pick something and go (I will talk about this more, later on in this chapter). The second is to look at your current and past client list. Do you see any patterns in the types of clients you work with? If you're a chiropractor, do you notice that a lot of your clients are golfers? If so, you could specialize in helping golfers, essentially specializing in the golf niche. If you're a life coach, are most of your clients recently divorced? If so, you could specialize in helping those who are divorced and in transition. If you're a small business attorney, are most of your clients family-owned businesses passed down from generation to generation? Are most of your clients concentrated in one type of industry? Whatever the answer is, that is a niche you can choose to focus on.

If you don't see obvious trends within your current and past clients, you may have to dig a little deeper below the surface. Recently, I taught a class on marketing to a local Chamber of Commerce group. I was speaking on this very subject—how to find a niche—when a young gentleman in the class, who was a mortgage broker, raised his hand. He told me that there was no way he could find a niche within his current and past clients because, in his words, "My clients are all across the board." I pressed him to look below the surface and dig deeper. "Are your clients mostly men or women?" "Women," he said. "Okay, good. Are those women married or divorced?" "I'd say, most are divorced." "Great. Keep going. Do they have kids?" "That's kind of split 50-50." "Okay, let's keep going. Have these divorced women ever purchased a home before?" "Most of them have not. Nearly all of the divorced women I help are first time home buyers."

Ding, ding, ding! We have a winner! I said, "Guess what? You're sitting on a niche that you could profit from and become well-known in. That niche would be helping recently divorced women purchase their first home. You could do so much with this niche. You could market your company as *the* mortgage company that knows and understands the emotions, stress, heartaches and headaches that recently divorced women face when trying to buy their first home after the break-up of their marriage. You could partner with a few divorce attorneys who could refer clients to you. These referrals would be a natural progression, once you have made a name for yourself. And most people probably know at least one divorced woman they could refer you to."

The light went on in his head. He got it, and he got really excited about it. The entire class did. That is the power of a niche—excitement, vision, and enthusiasm. There's not much excitement with the "anyone, everyone and someone" most small businesses use to define their target market.

Three 'Musts' Your Niche MUST Have

When choosing your niche, there are three "musts" the niche must have. They are:

Must #1

Your niche *must* have a history of wanting and buying the service or services you are offering. If your niche has never bought the type of service you offer, they probably won't just magically start. Find another niche who has bought and will continue to buy the service you provide.

Must #2

Your niche *must* be easy to find and market to. In order to market to a niche, you must know where they are and how to reach them. If you cannot locate the niche you have chosen, find another niche. At the bare minimum, you must be able to find names and addresses of the niche you want to target.

Must #3

Your niche *must* be big enough to sustain you, meaning your niche must be large enough and have enough buying units for you to make a living. If not, find another niche. There are no hard and fast rules for how big a niche must be, so you may have to experiment a bit to see if there are enough people to make it worth your while.

What if You're a Brand New Solo Small Business?

So, how do you find a niche if you're just starting out—few or no clients, no patterns emerging and you don't have any history to learn from? The solution is quite simple—just decide on and pick a few types of clients you'd want to work with.

Maybe you're a bookkeeper with a passion for entrepreneurs. You could establish yourself as *the* bookkeeper for home-based business-es. You can even take it one step further and establish yourself as *the* bookkeeper for women-owned, home-based businesses. A personal trainer could focus on personal training for stay-at-home moms with very small children who can't make it to the gym. You could establish yourself as *the* trainer who comes to the house and gives mom a full-body workout while the baby is napping.

Think of your passion or your hobbies or simply a type of person you would like to work with. Is there a niche you can tap into that parallels your interests? Dig a little deeper, search a little harder, brainstorm a little longer, and you will find there is a niche out there just waiting for you to conquer.

But, I Need Clients Right Now!

I've talked about all of the pluses to finding a niche, focusing on that niche and becoming a specialist in that niche. But, what if you need clients now? What if you have to get business quickly or you'll have to dine on mac-'n-cheese and ramen noodles for breakfast, lunch and dinner?

I understand where you're coming from, and, believe me, I and many other small business owners were in exactly the same boat when we started our own small businesses. You open the doors and have to get something going quick.

The need for clients *now* makes a lot of solo small business owners panic and revert back to the comfort of "anyone, everyone and someone." It's easier to say and is usually the default marketing position, and in an attempt to cast your net far and wide, you feel like you'll gobble up more clients faster. That is simply not true.

You will attract clients much, much faster if you will—even in the panic of needing clients right now—focus on a niche. Take a deep breath and decide on one area to focus on. Remember the nutritionist, and how he was struggling until he focused on a niche? Break down the things you do—the services you provide—into smaller chunks, and decide how you can focus on one niche with pinpoint accuracy. Then attack your marketing from that angle.

Let me give you an example. Say you're struggling and need clients right now. You are a chiropractor and have decided you're going to call 30 people you know and ask for a referral to drum up business. Which phone call will work faster for you: calling and asking, "Do you know anyone you could refer me to?" or making a slight change and asking, "Do you know an athlete who complains of migraine headaches you could refer me to?" Did you catch the niche? That's right … athletes who suffer from migraines.

A small change in the words you use will make big changes in the amount of response you'll get. Ask the first way, and you won't get a good response. Ask the second way, and most people can think of someone for you.

Whether you're jam-packed with clients or need them immediately, whether you've been in business for years or for days, focusing on a niche is the fast way to increase profits and the bottom line of your solo small business.

For more information or to get even more help on choosing the most profitable and best niche for your solo small business, check out the resources in the Appendix. ◆

Key Concept

Find A Niche And You'll Get Rich: Most solo small business owners have limited time, limited resources and limited money for marketing. Does that sound familar? Because of this, you must find a niche to target or your marketing efforts will not generate as great of success as possible. It's no longer okay to say you work with, "Anyone, everyone and someone ..." It's now time to pick a niche and focus on that niche. I have seen time and time again, solo small business owners who make this one seemingly minor shift (to actually focus on a niche) and it completely changes the success of their business. It really is *that* powerful!

Speak the Language of Results

One of the absolute key elements in marketing is the language you use to describe what you do. There are thousands, if not hundreds of thousands, of others out there who offer the same services you do. So how do you distinguish yourself? How do you move prospects to find out more about you versus someone else?

The Language of Your Prospect

The secret weapon is to speak the language of your prospect—which is the language of results. Most small businesses use the wrong language when speaking to prospects, and it just sits flat in their prospects' ears. Prospects have no idea how to respond to what they're hearing. If you don't speak your prospects' language, they'll be confused and won't respond the way you want.

The way to speak the language of results is:
1. Answer their questions and put their needs first,
2. Deal with their pain, problem or predicament,
3. Speak to their emotions, and
4. Avoid labels.

The Big Question

The language of results focuses first around one big question ... THE big question: *What's in it for me?* That's the big question that all prospects have in their minds. They may not consciously be aware of it, but it's there.

Remember the cold, hard truth? Prospects don't care about you; they only care about themselves, and they want to know—they demand to know—"What's in it for me?" That is the question you *must* answer, first and foremost. Don't say, "We are the oldest and best in our industry in the Dallas Metro area ..." "I have a degree in Psychology and Human Development from Stanford University ..." or "We have been in business for over 15 years ...." Those are wonderful things, but, 'What's in it for me?' is the big question every prospect has, and it is the first question you must answer.

Think about yourself for a moment. Who would you rather do business with, a small business owner who immediately addresses your needs or one who goes on and on about her qualifications before explaining how she can help you? It's like going into the electronics store for a stereo system that will give you the roundest, fullest, deepest bass sound for your jazz music and having the sales clerk tell you all about the fabulous training the store gave him. Big deal. Do you really care? No, you just want to know what's in it for you? "If I buy stereo X, will I get all of the benefits I want?"

Yes, qualifications, years in business, awards, customer service, credentials are great, fabulous and very important, but they belong at the end of your presentation, not the beginning.

Beyond the Big Question

The big question, "What's in it for me?" can also look like other questions that a prospect may throw at you. But, they're all manifestations of the big question … just said or thought in a slightly different way. Here are some common ones you may run into:

➤ Why should I care?

➤ What makes you different?

➤ Why should I trust and hire you?

➤ What makes you the expert?

Simply keep in mind that "What's in it for me?" is what the prospect wants to know. Fail to answer this question and you lose, game over, goodnight.

Pain, Problem or Predicament ... The 3P Approach

Most prospects work with service businesses because they have a pain, problem or predicament they need eased, solved or fixed. Prospects also may work with you because they wish to gain in some way, but, usually—more times than not—there's a pain, problem or predicament. Their marriage is close to ruin, so they need counseling to solve this problem. They suffer from low back pain, so they need you, a massage therapist, to alleviate the pain. They can't seem to find a career that suits them, so they need you, a career and personal coach, to guide them into the career that will give them fulfillment and solve the predicament of working in a job versus having a career.

To turn prospects into clients, you must focus on pain, problem or predicament.

Why is pain, problem or predicament so powerful? Consider this example: say you cut your foot while working in your garden. When you get to the hospital, do you want the ER doctor to begin by telling you he was on the honor roll in medical school or that he never skipped a class? No. You want him to look at your problem (your foot) and tell you what he can to do ease your pain (the cut) and fix your problem. The 3P approach is very effective, because it focuses on your prospects' needs and benefits.

Ease their pain, solve their problem or fix their predicament, and prospects become clients.

It's So Emotional

A fundamental principle to remember in marketing your small business is a principle we all know from basic sales training, which is: people buy emotionally, but justify their purchases logically. Don't believe me? Do you really think someone should buy one of those mega-size, monster-truck style SUVs? I mean, it borders on insanity to own a vehicle that seemingly can eat smaller cars for breakfast. Get hit by one of these things and it feels like a speed bump. A city dweller or suburbanite does not need a monster-mega-size SUV. It is completely illogical, but oh, so emotional. They're big, they're cool, they make a statement, they show you have money, and for guys, well … it's all emotional, not logical. If people bought logically, everyone would be driving the smallest, most fuel-efficient cars available.

When you market your small business, you have to speak to your prospects' emotions. If you do, you'll reap more profits and attract more clients.

You have to push your prospects' emotional hot buttons. The more buttons you hit, the better. When you discuss the pain, problem or predicament with your prospect, speak on a level of emotion. Quite simply, get out of your head and into your heart.

Here are some examples of speaking the language of emotion to a prospect:

> ➤ A massage therapist could talk about relieving chronic migraines that don't go away, no matter how many pain pills you pop.
> ➤ A chiropractor could talk about relieving excruciating back pain that keeps you from being as active as you want to be.
> ➤ A physical therapist could talk about alleviating stiff and sore muscles and joints so you can work in your garden again.
> ➤ A marriage counselor could talk about saving a marriage of over 28 years that has slowly had the life sucked out of it and how you can rekindle lost flames.

These are emotional issues. They get to the heart of the situation and directly address the reason why a prospect should work with you. Once you hit the emotion and prospects become clients, they will justify their purchase logically.

Emotional:
"I have chronic migraines and no matter how many pain pills I take, they don't go away."

Logical:
"These massage therapy sessions are $65 per hour, but it is totally worth it to get rid of the headaches."

I do the same thing when I buy, and you do the same thing when you buy. We all do. That's just how people work. Think about it: do you really need an Apple iPod®? Sure, you may want it, but do you really *need* it? Of course not. But they're cool, they're hip and they hold a truckload of songs. All of this is emotional. When you buy, you justify the purchase logically. "Well, if I buy an iPod, I can listen to informative audio books in my car. I can eliminate the hassle of having to change CDs. It will keep me from getting bored on long road trips" … all justifications in a logical manner.

Enough with the Labels

The final point of the language of results is avoiding labels. There are two reasons for this. One, labels are generalizations. When you describe yourself, your services or your potential clients with labels, it's like saying "anyone, everyone and someone." Two, labels are logical, not emotional. Labels are not specific enough—or emotional enough—to trigger the responses you want.

A typical example of this is how you answer the question, "What do you do for a living?" It's a question we're asked all the time. Typical responses are: "I'm a graphic designer," "I'm an architect," or "I'm an accountant." If this is how you answer this question, you're labeling yourself. You are *not* a label. You are a professional and expert in solving a prospect's pain, problem or predicament. You have to answer questions like this in the language of results.

I could answer the "What do you do for a living?" question with, "I'm a graphic designer, web designer and marketing consultant." Snooze. Boring. There are a million graphic designers. There are a million web designers, and there are a million marketing consultants. Whoopee. Who cares?

That answer isn't effective, because it's a label. It's general instead of specific, and logical instead of emotional. When people ask me what I do, I reply:

> "I help solo small business owners who are phenomenal at what they do, but are struggling in their business because their marketing isn't working effectively and they can't seem to attract enough clients."

Did you notice the emotional words? "Phenomenal," "struggling," "isn't working," "can't seem to attract" …. It's a very emotional description, and when I answer this way to prospects who are in this very situation themselves, it immediately leads into their next question, which is always, "Really? How do you do that?" This happens no less than eight times out of ten, simply because it's specific and emotional. It hits the prospects' buttons and makes them want to know more. ◆

Key Concept

The Language of Your Prospect: The language of your prospect is emotion and results. To speak this language you need to: focus on answering their questions (especially the big questions of "What's in it for me?", "What makes you different?", "Why should I care?", "What makes you the expert?", etc.) and putting their needs first. You also need to deal with their 3Ps (pain, problem or predicament) and always remember people buy emotionally ... there is emotion in everything. And last avoid using labels when you describe your business and the services you provide.

Delivering Your Message

Now that we understand the language of results, let's put it to work to create two very useful tools that will help you deliver your message to prospects: the Situation/Solution Summary™ and the "What Do You Do?" Commercial™.

The Situation/Solution Summary™

The best tool to communicate the prospect's 3Ps—pain, problem or predicament—is the one-page Situation/Solution Summary™, which is just what it sounds like: a summary of the situations you can deal with and the solution(s) you can and will provide.

I first learned about this incredible little tool from Robert Middleton* of Action Plan Marketing. (If you haven't heard of Robert, you're

---

*Robert Middleton, Action Plan Marketing, www.ActionPlan.com.

definitely missing out. Robert is an incredibly knowledgeable marketing guru. He taught me how to create what he calls an Executive Summary. It's Robert's teaching on this topic that helped me create the Situation/Solution Summary™.)

The summary is simple to create, yet very powerful. Once you create your Summary, you can use it in practically any marketing piece. The Summary is where I start with just about every one of my clients. Once its created, we take the Summary—in whole or in parts—and use it on a website, as a basis for brochure copy, as a foundation for a direct mail campaign, and even to incorporate elements into a "What Do You Do?" Commercial™.

There are seven steps in creating a Situation/Solution Summary™. They are:

1. Create an attention-getting, 3P-related headline.
2. Talk about the prospect's pain, problem or predicament.
3. Paint a perfect picture of when the pain, problem or predicament is solved.
4. Describe the stumbling block or what's getting in the prospect's way.
5. Present the perfect solution.
6. Sing your own praises.
7. Provide a call to action.

The reason the Situation/Solution Summary™ is so powerful is because it focuses first and foremost on the prospect—which should sound familiar from the other chapters you've read—and then gradually moves through the steps, leading the prospect through his Situation and ending at you as the Solution, as illustrated in Figure 1.

SITUATION/SOLUTION SUMMARY™

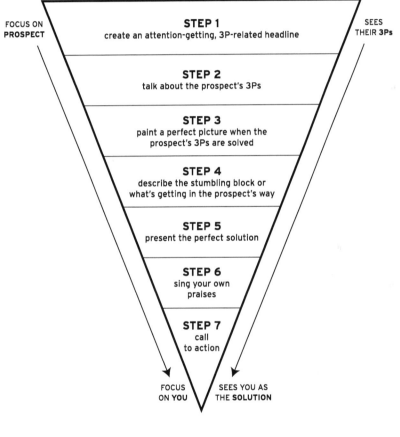

FIGURE 1

It's time to fire up Microsoft® Word or some other trusty word processing program and create a Summary for your small business.

Step 1: Create an Attention-Getting, 3P-Related Headline

Start off with a headline that asks a question related to the 3Ps—pain, problem or predicament. The purpose of this headline is to really pique the interest of your prospects. You want them to sit up and take notice. You want them to see themselves and think, "Yeah, this relates to me." You must interest them in reading more.

Headlines are not an exact science. You have to test and experiment with a number of headlines before you find the one(s) that really ring true with your prospects. The best place to start is by listening to your clients. What pain, problem or predicament do they talk about? Simply take that and use it as your 3P-related headline.

An example I often use is:

Struggling to Attract More Clients on a Consistent Basis?

This headline is simply something taken from what I hear my clients and prospects express all the time. I just use what I hear. Because my target market wants to solve this predicament (attracting clients consistently), I know this headline will pique their attention. You should develop your headline exactly the same way.

This headline focuses on the pain, problem, or predicament. But what if your target audience wants to gain, which is sometimes the case? How do you write a "gain" headline?

Here are some examples of 'gain' headlines:

➤ Ready to Shave 5 Strokes Off Your Golf Game?

➤ How Would You Like to Increase Your Renewal Commissions by 65%?

➤ Tired of Getting Only 5-6% Return from Your Investments?

Notice that the shift is quite subtle between a pain, problem or predicament headline and a gain headline. If you really think about it, a gain headline is just another pain, problem or predicament, written in a slightly different tone. Don't make this hard. Simply think about what your prospect wants to do: get out of pain, solve a problem, fix a predicament or gain something, and write your headline to match.

Step 2: Talk About the Prospect's 3Ps – Pain, Problem or Predicament

Next, talk about the pain, problem or predicament. Do this by making a combination of statements and questions relating to the prospect's pain, problem or predicament.

My example:

If you're like most solos small business owners, attracting enough clients on a consistent basis is hard work and takes up a lot of your time. You're probably so busy working with the clients you currently have that your marketing efforts usually get put on the back burner. When you do have time to market your services, are you frustrated with the results?

As you can see, this first section hits some emotional hot-buttons and targets the pain, problem or predicament that a lot of small business owners face. How did I know what to put in this first paragraph? Simply by listening and observing. I listened to the complaints of my prospects and watched what they struggle with again and again. From this info, I wrote.

Put yourself in your prospects' shoes. What are they struggling with? What keeps them up at night? What do they want to solve? These are the items you will want to focus on.

Step 3: Paint a Perfect Picture of When the Pain, Problem or Predicament is Solved

Next, paint a picture of how this same situation can and will be in a perfect world—the perfect world beginning once they have hired you to help them.

My example:

You can attract all the clients you want and can handle. You can market your business successfully. It is possible to get off of the "feast or famine" roller-coaster of inconsistent marketing results and inconsistent clients. It is possible to have all of your marketing materials be very effective. And it is possible to have your pipeline consistently filled with new clients ready to work with you.

This is a very rosy picture, but not far-fetched. Don't be modest here. Tell your prospect exactly what can and will happen. This gives the prospect a view into the future. The first paragraph was what your prospects are dealing with; this paragraph is where your prospects can be once it's dealt with.

Step 4: Describe the Stumbling Block or What's Getting in the Prospect's Way

Next, tell prospects why they haven't already solved their pain, problem or predicament. What's happening in their world that has prevented them from moving forward? Maybe it's fear. Maybe it's lack of knowledge. Whatever it is, this is where you focus on it.

My example:

If it's so easy, then why haven't you done it? Most solos small business owners are really good at what they do, but not so good at marketing their services. It's no wonder your pipeline eventually dries up. Once you do get clients, you are usually so focused on working with those clients that your marketing efforts take a back seat. The results: inconsistency, low income and frustration. It really is a vicious cycle that seems impossible to get out of.

Step 5: Present the Perfect Solution

So far, you've told your prospects what their pain, problem or predicament is. You've told them how great life can be once they fix things. Then you empathized with them and illustrated that you understand why they have not already solved this pain, problem or predicament. Now it's time to tell them what they need to do.

My example:

Smart and successful solo small business owners turn to outside help for effective marketing solutions. The best investment you can make in your business is to work with an expert who knows how to market your business in a way that ensures success. Smart and successful solo business owners know they can't do everything themselves. By working with an expert, you can focus on what you do best—servicing your existing clients—while your business is being marketed consistently and successfully. The results: attract all the clients you want and can handle, increase your income and no longer struggle to fill your pipeline on a consistent basis.

Step 6: Sing Your Own Praises

Now for the fun part: you get to sing your own praises. This is where you and your expertise get to shine. Prove to your prospects that you are the very best person to hire.

My example:

Jeanna Pool has the experience, expertise and tools to make you more successful. Jeanna Pool of www.MarketingFor Solos.com has been helping solo small businesses attract more clients for over 15 years. Jeanna helps solo small business owners by creating and executing comprehensive marketing programs that really work, marketing consulting and coaching, as well as, conducting seminars and workshops and authoring a variety of books and programs to teach solo small business owners how to market their services successfully.

Step 7: Provide a Call to Action

The last step is to invite prospects to pick up the phone and give you a call. If you also offer a free gift of some sort—free trial, demo, example, consultation, etc., mention that, too.

My example:

To learn more about how Jeanna can help you start attracting more clients, please visit her website at www.MarketingFor Solos.com. Jeanna works with a limited number of private clients. To learn more, she offers qualified solo small business owners a 30-minute free consultation to discuss how she can help you generate stellar results from all of your marketing activities and efforts.

That's it: the Situation/Solution Summary™ in seven simple steps. Once you've written your summary, print it out on a sheet of your letterhead. To start with, you can use this as a handout describing your services, or expand it into a brochure or other marketing piece. The possibilities for this simple and powerful tool are endless, but the best thing about the Summary is, after a short time of writing it, you'll be amazed how effective it is.

The "What Do You Do?" Commercial™

Now, let's take a closer look at your answer to the question, "What do you do?" You need to have your answer ready. It needs to have a strong dose of emotional hot-buttons and has to use the language of results.

Your answer to this question is what different people call an audio logo, an elevator speech, a 15-second commercial and many other names. I like to call it simply the "What Do You Do?" Commercial™. There have been a number of books written about how to develop a good commercial. I'm going to give you my take on the subject.

What is a Commercial?

A commercial is a very short, but detailed, emotionally-targeted description of the main thing you do for your clients.

Here are a few examples:

➤ "I help overworked and overwhelmed small business owners better manage their time to get all of the things on their 'to do' list done."

➤ "I work with 40-somethings who are completely fed up with their 'jobs' and want to find their life's passion in work."

➤ "I work with seniors who suffer from constant chronic pain and fatigue feel more energized to lead active and exhilarating lives."

Do you hear the emotion in these commercials? That's what makes them work—emotion. It's not sappy, over-the-top emotion, but emotion that hits on the issue central to the prospect's struggle.

Constructing a Successful Commercial

There are two parts to a successful "What Do You Do?" Commercial™—Part One: The Beginning and Part Two: The Clincher.

Part One: The Beginning, contains 3 key elements:

1. The niche you work with (you are going to find a niche and specialize in that niche, now aren't you?),
2. Emotional words that describe that niche's pain, problem or predicament, and
3. A glimpse of how you will solve that niche's pain, problem or predicament.

You don't want to give away too much at the beginning of your commercial. The beginning is just to hit the emotional hot-buttons and tell your prospect the answer to the all important question, "What's in it for me?"

Here's Part One: The Beginning of my commercial:

"I help solo small business owners who are really good at what they do, but struggle with their marketing and can't seem to attract enough clients consistently."

A successful Part One: The Beginning of your commercial is one that ...

➤ Is short. Don't go on and on and on. You should be able to say it in no more than one, two or at the very most three short sentences. You want to pique the interest of your prospects, not lull them to sleep with a dissertation.

➤ Uses emotional words. Choose your words carefully. You want to hit on your prospects' issues without going overboard. Get into the hearts of your prospects. What do they struggle with? What keeps them up at night? What is their pain, problem or predicament? Highlight this in your commercial.

➤ Leads the prospect to ask the all-important next question, "How do you do that?"

If, after speaking your commercial, the prospect doesn't ask, "How do you do that?", it's time to go back to the drawing board and develop a different commercial. A good commercial will get the prospect to ask this next question at least eight out of ten times.

Once you've successfully delivered Part One: The Beginning of your commercial, and your prospects know what's in it for them and have asked, "How do you do that?" (or some other variant of this question), it's time to move on to Part Two: The Clincher of your commercial.

Part Two: The Clincher also contains 3 key elements:

1. A restatement of the niche's pain, problem or predicament,
2. A snapshot of how you solve or address the niche's pain, problem or predicament, and
3. A snapshot of the results and benefits the niche gets by working with you.

Part Two: The Clincher is a wrap-up of your commercial and should motivate prospects to want to find out much more about what you do. It can move prospects to ask you more in-depth questions, discuss their situation with you or, in the perfect world, get them to set up an appointment with you to discuss the possibility of working together.

Here's Part Two: The Clincher of my commercial:

The prospect asks, "How do you do that?" I answer with:

"Well, most solo small businesses struggle with their marketing and attracting clients consistently (a restatement of the niche's pain, problem or predicament) because they're experts in their field, not experts at marketing. So one of the things I do is, come in as their internal marketing department, to develop and handle all of their marketing, so their business is marketed successfully—which attracts clients consistently (a snapshot of how I solve or address the niche's pain, problem or predicament). In turn, they get to do what they do best and love, which is working with their existing clients, rather than having to struggle and fumble to figure out how to market themselves (a snapshot of the results and benefits that the niche gets by working with me).”

The goal of the clincher is to give prospects enough information to continue to ask questions, move closer to finding out more and consider working with you.

To wrap up, here is my “What Do You Do?” Commercial™ in its completed form; Part One: The Beginning and Part Two: The Clincher:

"Jeanna, what do you do?"

“I help solo small business owners who are really good at what they do, but struggle with their marketing and can’t seem to attract enough clients consistently.”

"How do you do that?"

“Most solo small businesses struggle with attracting clients consistently because they’re experts in their field, but not experts at marketing. So one of the things I do is, come in as their internal marketing department, to develop and handle all of their marketing activites, so their business is marketed in a successful and effective manner—which attracts clients consistently. In turn, they get to do what they do best and love, which is working with their existing clients, rather than having to struggle and fumble to figure out how to market themselves.”

Keep in mind that you can have several commercials in your arsenal. The commercial I just shared with you is only for one aspect of my business, which is being hired as the internal marketing department for a few solo small business owners. At other times and at other events, I may highlight a different service I provide. In fact, I have between five and seven different commercials in my arsenal, ready to use when I want to market a different service I offer. But, all of my commercials follow exactly the same format as the example above. You can and should do the same for your business.

Swing and a Miss

A mistake that a lot of small business owners make with their commercials is trying to hit a grand slam with the prospect. It's because of this that many solo small business owners fall back into describing themselves with a label—accountant, business coach, lawyer, chiropractor, massage therapist, etc.—when asked the all important question, "What do you do?"

You may think that once you deliver this impeccable, stellar commercial, your prospect will say, "Wow! This is exactly what I've been searching for all of my life. I have a $3 million dollar budget. Can I write you a check right now so we can get started?!" That just ain't gonna happen (although it sure would be nice, wouldn't it?).

Don't swing so big and so hard that you strike out when delivering your commercial. The goal—in fact the *only* goal of your commercial—is simply to pique your prospects' interest and inspire them to find out more. Then, slowly but surely, you'll move them along your sales process to becoming a client.

For more information and help to construct a client-attracting What Do You Do? Commercial™ for your solo small business, check out the resources in the Appendix. ◆

Market LESS To Be More Successful

A mistake that a lot of solo small business owners make is not being focused enough with their marketing efforts and marketing activities.

Many solos struggle to attract clients on a consistent basis because they're scattered in their efforts and easily get distracted by all of the marketing activities and options available to them. Most solo small businesses jump from activity to activity to activity, and try a little bit of everything, or anything possible when it comes to the marketing of their services.

To combat this problem, I'm going to teach you how to market *less* in order to be more successful. What I'm about to teach you is revolutionary and will completely change your marketing mindset and outlook. A lot of people teach, you should do as much as possible for marketing. That may work for some businesses, but as solos, doing everything only leads to frustration, confusion, overwhelm and lack of results. As I just mentioned this is one of the reasons so many solos really struggle to attract clients consistently … they're too scattered and try to do way too much. As solos we only have so much time and therefore we must really focus our efforts.

I'm going to teach you a method for choosing the right marketing tools and activities to help you focus. This is one of the core principles of the Marketing for Solos System™. It's based on *the principle of strategic diversification.*

Strategic Diversification

Strategic diversification is the happy medium between not doing enough for marketing versus trying to do too much. The point is to diversify your efforts, but not too widely, and in a consistent, focused way. In other words, you should employ more than one marketing tool or activity, but not too many.

Why Strategically Diversify?

There are three big reasons why you should strategically diversify your marketing tools and activities:

First …

Strategic diversification prevents a complete loss of business if a marketing avenue slows down or dries up completely.

There are a lot of solo small business owners who do not strategically diversify their marketing activities. Their marketing efforts focus on one area and one area only. They put all of their eggs into one basket. This is a meltdown just waiting to happen. Let me explain.

Whenever I ask solo small business owners how they get clients, what do you think the number one answer is 99% of the time? Yep, you guessed it: referrals. When I ask them *what else* they do to get clients, 99% of the time the answer is, "That's all, just referrals, we don't really do anything else."

What these solos don't realize is: failure to diversify their small business' marketing activities is like failing to diversify their retirement portfolio.

What are they going to do when the one-and-only area they are completely focusing on—referrals—slows down or completely dries up? Can you say crash and burn? It's like putting all of your money in one type of stock and the company goes broke.

This is why you need to diversify your marketing activities. You *never* want to focus on just one marketing activity. Diversify your marketing activities to prevent a complete loss of new clients if and when one area slows down. The bottom line is you will *always* experience slow times in your business. If you're not diversified, what in the world are you going to do when the slow times come? And come they will, I guarantee it.

Just like a diversified retirement portfolio, a diversified marketing portfolio is the safe and smart route to long-term success. Diversifying gives you options. Diversifying gives you outlets. Diversifying gives you other avenues to find new clients when the slow times come. Diversifying prevents a total crash and burn if and when a marketing activity slows down or completely dries up.

Second ...

Strategic diversification is a focused approach that is manageable, doable and makes good use of your very limited and very precious time. Bottom line: it gets rid of the overwhelm factor.

When your a solo small business, you are, after all, only one person. And, more than likely, you don't have a staff. If you do have a staff, that's a huge bonus, but typically they work part-time or their time is focused on things other than marketing. More often than not, everything is on your shoulders. You are the President and CEO, the accounting and finance person, the human resources department, the sales department, the marketing department, the administrative assistant, janitor, and, oh yes, the one who must *actually* do the work for clients!

Strategically diversifying—following a few marketing paths, but not too many—keeps you from being so overwhelmed by the potential activities that you do nothing, or freeze because you don't know what to do and where to start. It gives you a few activities to focus on and master.

It's like working out at the gym. There are dozens of possibilities: stair climbers, treadmills, stationary bikes, rowing machines, dumbbells, barbells, and on and on. The options and possibilities are overwhelming, but when you focus on a core group of exercises, you'll get results much faster than floating around the gym trying a little bit of everything. If you ever work out with a personal trainer, they'll give you a set number of exercises to do. They strategically diversify your workout. They vary things so you won't get bored, but there is a limited amount of different tools used, so you get the most out of the exercises you do.

Third ...

Strategic diversification ensures that you hit prospects in different ways, avenues and methods.

People, including prospects, learn and take in information in many different ways. Think about it for a moment: how do you learn something new? Do you read something once and get it? Do you have to read it, do it and read it again? Do you learn only by doing? Do you learn only be seeing? Do you learn only by listening?

If you fail to diversify your marketing materials and marketing activities, then you're presenting prospects with only one way to take in the information you want them to learn—essentially you're forcing them to learn it your way. But, if it's not the way they learn, they won't take it in, and they won't hire you.

For example, if you only have a small, tri-fold brochure with five to ten bullet points of information about your small business and this is the marketing tool you give to prospects, you're essentially saying, "This is it, take it or leave it. Either you understand my business by reading this one marketing piece I have for you or you don't. If you don't have enough information, sorry; I have nothing else to give you." Do you see how this can be a problem?

Different marketing tools and activities speak to different prospects in different ways. You have to speak to prospects in the way they understand, learn and take in information the best.

How Much Do I Diversify?

Okay, you know and understand why you should strategically diversify your marketing tools and activities, so now the question becomes, "How much do I diversify?"

A lot of sales and marketing consultants teach that you should try to do absolutely everything possible to market and reach your target. I disagree. As a solo, one of the main challenges you have is time. Is there enough time in the day, week, month and year to get everything done? I'd say no. We have too many things to do and focus on, thus a "do everything possible" approach is simply too overwhelming and too time-consuming. Solo small businesses that think they must market themselves this way freeze and do nothing—because they know there is no possible way they can do everything.

If you've ever felt the overwhelm of trying to do everything, just take a look at the illustration in Figure 2 on Page 70 and it's pretty easy to see why this is such a problem.

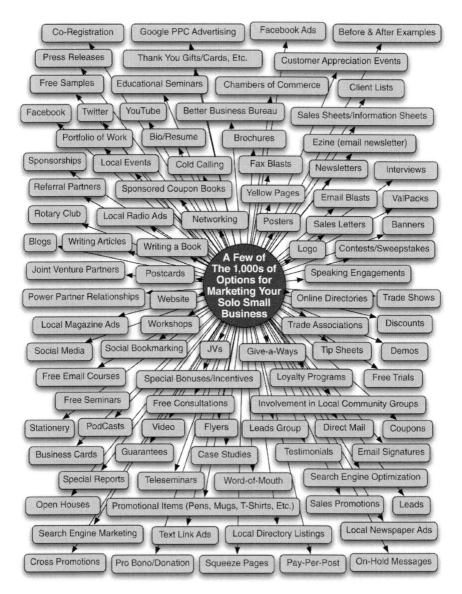

FIGURE 2

Is it any wonder why you feel overwhelmed and freeze when it comes to choosing
the marketing tools and activities for your solo small business?

The solution is to choose between three and six tools or activities to focus on. You don't want less than three, or you will not have enough diversified activity to reach different people in different ways. You do not want many more than six, or you'll get too overwhelmed to keep up with them. The happy medium is three to six.

Now, only three to six activities may not seem like a lot, but believe me—when your small business is you and as a solo—with all the projects, clients, tasks and other items vying for your time, you'll quickly come to know that three to six is a good and manageable number.

Here are the marketing tools I use for my own solo small business ...

1. A Comprehensive, Workhorse Website™.

My website has a ton of information about the 3Ps many of my prospects face. The site also has information about how I work, the results I achieve for my clients and much, much more. My website gives prospects all of the information they want and need to make a decision about working with me. It works very well for those prospects who have to read and digest a lot of information before making a decision. I talk more about this is Chapter 8.

2. Writing articles and publishing an eZine (email newsletter).

I write a lot of articles and have an email newsletter. This illustrates to prospects my expertise and knowledge of marketing-related, graphic design and website design issues that I know how to solve.

3. A referral/networking group.

I am an active member of a formal referral group called BNI—Business Network International. I'll talk more about BNI later. BNI focuses on passing quality word-of-mouth referrals among its members.

4. Speaking engagements and workshops.

I speak on marketing-related topics to both small and large groups, and conduct workshops on various marketing topics. This lets me share my knowledge and expertise with the audience—which, of course, are my prospects and potential clients—and gives them a taste of how I may be able to help them.

5. Direct mail.

I am a big believer in direct mail, especially direct mail postcards. I talk more about this in Chapter 8. I mail direct mail postcards to prospects usually monthly or, at the very least, bi-monthly to generate new business.

These are the marketing tools and activities that I use on a regular basis. I use a few others from time to time, but these are my main focus. Your combination can be anything you want it to be.

Keep these things in mind when choosing the tools and activities for your small business ...

➤ Make sure the marketing tools and activities you choose fit within your personality. If you have a hard time speaking in front of people, then speaking engagements or workshops may not be the best fit for you. This may seem obvious, but I see a lot of solo small business owners trying to push themselves into activities that are just not right for them. There are many tools and activities to choose from: choose those you'll actually do and enjoy.

➤ Make sure that the tools and activities you choose fit with the way your prospective clients shop for and find services in your industry. For example, Yellow Page advertising doesn't work very well for my industry. Most of the prospects I'm targeting don't look for my type of services in the Yellow Pages. So, I'm better served putting the money that I would spend on a Yellow Page ad into some other tool or activity. Look at your prospects. How do they find businesses that offer what you do? That's probably a tool or activity you need to be involved with.

➤ Make sure that the tools and activities you choose are ones you can continue, focus on and master. You need to *strategically* diversify—choose wisely the tools you'll use—so you'll have time to employ and manage your marketing efforts. Choose a combination of tools and activities that you can and will be devoted to. It will do you no good to choose three to six tools or activities and then do nothing or start and then abruptly stop.

Once you have mastered these three to six tools and activities that you choose to focus on, and the clients are rolling in, then and only then should you and *can* you add more tools to your arsenal.

The key is to keep marketing manageable, doable and sustainable. Many solo small businesses fail because they try to do too much and are so overwhelmed by the amount of marketing tasks they can never keep up. Focusing on a little at a time will go a very, very long way.

Passive Versus Active Marketing, a Key Component of Strategic Diversification

Far too many solo small business owners are *passive* in their approach to marketing. They just sit in their office and wait for the phone to ring. When someone asks, "How do you get clients?" they always say, "Referrals." Now, referrals are fantastic—I love referrals—but way too many solos rely totally and completely on referrals. Not only that, but they have absolutely no *active* way to generate referrals. They just sit and wait for referrals to call or come knocking.

If this sounds like the way you market your small business, it's time for a change. This is a totally *passive* approach. Your marketing is not in your control—and that's a mistake. You *must* have a good mix of active and passive marketing tools.

Active tools are those you take an active approach in, such as speaking, workshops, writing articles, and networking. You are actively doing the marketing activity. You don't just "set it and forget it" (to borrow a phrase from Ron Popeil) and thus have active control in your marketing.

Passive tools are those where the tool or activity itself is working rather than you, and since they don't change very much, these slant more toward "set it and forget it." Examples are brochures, flyers, advertising, etc. Even though you were active in creating these materials, the materials are actually doing the work and helping to attract clients to you. You may or may not be face to face with prospects when they see your brochure, hence it's doing the work and it's a passive tool.

Make sure you have a good mix of both. I counsel my clients that a bare minimum breakdown is 70-30, meaning … 70% of your marketing tools and activities are active and 30% are passive. You can adjust this percentage to your liking (75% active, 25% passive, 80% active, 20% passive, etc.); however, make sure that you have at least 70% of your marketing tools and activities *active,* or you're marketing isn't in your control.

For your convenience, I've created a list of active and passive marketing tools and activities. Simply visit: www.MarketingForSolos .com/book-gift and there you can download the "Active and Passive Marketing Tools Worksheet."

Final Thoughts on Strategic Diversification of Your Marketing Tools and Activities

We talked about the minimum breakdown between active and passive marketing activities, but now we need to go even further in our diversification. Take a look at where the majority of your new clients are coming from. You should be diversified enough so that no *one* marketing activity—active or passive—generates more than 50% of your new clients. For example, if you get 90% of your new clients via referrals, you need to diversify your activities so that you get new clients 50% of the time or less via referrals and the other 50% spread out between the other two to six marketing activities.

Again, strategic diversification is insurance against one tool or activity drying up and leaving you in a major panic for clients. ◆

 Key Concept

Strategic Diversification: The way to end being scattered in your marketing efforts and to keep from feeling overwhelmed by all of the options available, is to choose between 3 to 6 marketing tools and activities to focus on. This strategically diversifies your efforts and makes marketing manageable and doable, even as a solo. Remember to choose more active activities than passive ones, so you can be in control of your marketing and the results you achieve.

CHAPTER

Choosing the RIGHT Marketing Tools and Activities

Over the past few chapters, we've talked about focusing on the prospect first and you last, changing your thinking, finding your best target or niche, speaking the language of results and emotion, focusing your efforts and incorporating strategic diversification so that you can market less and be more successful …

Now, it's time to talk about choosing the right marketing tools and activities for the job.

The following tools and activities are proven methods for marketing solo small businesses that provide a service to their clients. You do not market a service-based business the same way you market a product-based business—it just doesn't work. A product is a tangible, viewable and touchable item. Services are intangible or "invisible" to the prospect. When you're "selling" an intangible item— a service—your prospects make the decision to hire you based on *you:* your knowledge, empathy and understanding of the prospect's pain, problem or predicament, your expertise in your field and the results you have achieved for past clients and thus will achieve for new clients.

Here are the most effective tools and activities for marketing your solo small business.

Logo, Stationery and a Professional Image

You may wonder why I listed a logo, stationery and a professional image as tools or activities to focus on in marketing. I did because your logo and professional image are the absolute, fundamental first step to success in your solo small business.

I don't care if you've been in business two-days or 20-years, your logo is the face of your small business. Your logo is the first impression that everyone sees and judges you by. Your logo will either say you're an expert who is a professional and worth the price you charge for your services, or it will say you're an amateur who doesn't really care what you look like and are not worth the time.

Your logo is absolutely *that* important.

There is a mistake that I see a lot of small business owners make. It's the mistake of having your logo, stationery and the image of your small business look cheap and unprofessional.

This is a very costly mistake that, unfortunately, most solo small businesses do not understand. They don't realize how much damage they are doing to their business by using an unprofessional identity. Essentially, what they're doing is creating a sub-par first impression that will be burned into the minds of new prospects forever.

The old adage is true: you never get a second chance to make a first impression. When running a small business, you cannot afford to look cheap or unprofessional. You must stand out from the crowd. You must look different. You must show the world that you care enough to invest in a professionally designed logo and stationery, and have a professional image that conveys that you are, in fact, a professional.

If you don't look professional, if you look amateurish, a few things will happen. Prospects will pass on your products or services and go to your competitors. You will not earn the price you are worth. You will not be trusted as the very best in your field. Prospects will view and judge you as someone you are not. You will have a very hard time building your reputation. Most important, you will lose money. Period.

What Image Can Do for Your Business

Image can make you look like the best, or the worst.

Think for a moment about Starbucks®. Its image is one of excellence and top quality in the world of coffee. Because of the image it has, we willingly pay far more money for coffee when we could go down the street, somewhere else and pay much less for the same thing. But, the Starbucks image says, "We are worth the price; we are the best." Starbucks has added to the success of its business by developing a professional, successful and quality image.

Image can make you look cheap, even if you don't want to look that way. I recently spoke to an owner of a small venture capital firm. His business is small, but he works with very large companies to secure them millions of dollars in financing. Yet, when I reviewed his logo, I found it to be absolutely atrocious. That may seem harsh, but let's not pull any punches here. It was atrocious. He did it himself by throwing together a font and some clip art that came with Microsoft® Word. A three-year-old may as well have designed it, because it looked that elementary and unprofessional.

Why in the world would potential clients trust his firm to handle millions of dollars in venture funding when his image did nothing to communicate his expertise and professionalism?

A successful image will help you attract the types of clients you want to work with. You will send the message that you're worth your price. You will convey the impression that you're the best in your industry. When you project the right image, you will give your prospects the sense that they would be crazy not to do business with you.

Your logo, stationery and professional image is the fundamental starting point for marketing success in your solo small business. If it's not in order first, all of your other tools and activities will be handicapped in their effectiveness.

Your brochure may speak the language of results, but if your logo and image are poor, prospects won't take you seriously. Your website may attract clients like a magnet because of your expertise in your industry, but if your image gives the impression of being cheap or unprofessional, prospects still won't believe that you really are the right person to hire.

Your logo, stationery and professional image are tools that must be perfected first. Make sure that each conveys the message you want.

Brochures and Collateral Materials

Your brochure and collateral materials (other physical, printed, marketing-related materials, such as flyers, presentation folders, sales sheets, etc.) are *very* powerful tools to help you attract more clients on a consistent basis.

These tools sell your services to prospective clients, demonstrate your expertise, demonstrate your professionalism and—most of all—convince prospective clients that your solo small business is *the* business to hire.

When you develop any brochures and collateral materials for your solo small business make sure that ...

➤ They speak the language of results and completely focus on the prospect first and foremost, and you last.

➤ They contain *enough* information to persuade prospects to find out more about you, rather than just a few sentences and some bullet points.

➤ They answer the prospect's BIG question: "What's in it for me?" That can also manifest itself as "Why should I care?" and "Why should I trust or hire you?"

➤ They focus on only *one* topic or aspect of your services at a time. Don't dilute the message by trying to cram everything you do into one brochure. Have a separate brochure for each service you provide. If you target more than one niche, have a separate brochure for each niche. This ensures that your prospect sees one focused message versus a brochure that looks like an overwhelming novel of every single thing you do. Keep the information focused on one subject, one aspect of the 3Ps, and on one niche at a time.

Let me give you an example of why focusing on only *one* topic or aspect of your services at a time is so *very* important. A client hired me to design a brochure for her interior design business to use as a giveaway and lead generation tool at a very large trade show she'd be attending. The trade show was for a very specific industry and niche. Potential clients at this show represented only one aspect of my client's interior design business.

I counseled her that the best strategy for this brochure was to focus on only the *one* specific area of her business that was the same focus for the trade show. In the brochure, we spoke only of the 3Ps of this very small and very specific niche. We only spoke of her services that related to this niche. We only listed past clients in this niche. We did not dilute the brochure by listing *any* other services she offered. The only services listed were those that these potential clients would use.

The brochure worked like a charm. After my client returned from the trade show, she said that prospects loved the brochure and thought that she was the only interior designer at the show who specialized in their niche.

Was my client the *only* interior designer at the show? Was my client the *only* interior designer who specializes in this particular niche? No. But, by focusing on only one topic and aspect of service in the brochure, it hit the prospects right between the eyes and positioned my client as the expert and "only interior designer" for this industry.

The Professional Touch

Unless your brochures and collateral materials are professionally designed and persuasively written—in a way that captures attention and lets your prospects know exactly why they should be doing business with you—they'll just sit there taking up space and won't produce the results you want.

When done correctly and professionally, brochures and collateral materials are small business marketing tools that will help you attract clients consistently over the life of your solo small business.

Comprehensive, Workhorse Website™

A comprehensive, workhorse website™ is an absolute must as a solo small business owner. I truly believe that a comprehensive, workhorse website, if developed correctly, can be *the most powerful* tool in your marketing arsenal. Notice that I did not say "a website." I said a *comprehensive, workhorse website.* There is a very big difference.

When designed correctly and effectively, a comprehensive, workhorse website can act as the central hub of your marketing efforts and attract clients to your solo small business like a magnet. It can and will do all of the heavy lifting for your marketing, just like a workhorse (hence the name). I have seen this happen again and again and again, with my comprehensive, workhorse website, and with those I've designed for my private clients.

Just a Website or a Comprehensive, Workhorse Website™ … What's the Difference?

There are five big differences between just a website and a comprehensive, workhorse website. They are:

Difference #1:

A *comprehensive, workhorse website* builds an entire case to convince clients to hire you by explaining and illustrating who you are, what you do and why someone should work with you versus your competition. A *website* is usually not much more than a few paragraphs, pages and bullet points. In reality, it's usually nothing more than a glorified brochure on the web.

Difference #2:

A *comprehensive, workhorse website* answers all possible questions that a prospect may have about you and what you offer. It leaves no question unanswered and no potential hesitation unaddressed. A *website* leaves too many questions unanswered in the prospects' minds. There is not enough information to build a case as to why a prospect should hire you. The prospect is left wanting much more and will go somewhere else—usually to your competition—to find it.

Difference #3:

A *comprehensive, workhorse website* motivates clients to pick up the phone and make contact with you. A *website* does absolutely nothing to motivate a prospect to pick up the phone and call you.

Difference #4:

A *comprehensive, workhorse website* shortens the sales cycle and sales process. A prospect who visits your website and then calls you already knows who you are, what you have to offer and how you can possibly help him. It does all the heavy lifting for you. A *website* does nothing to shorten the sales process. A prospect doesn't really know who you are and what you can do from visiting a website.

Difference #5:

A *comprehensive, workhorse website* actually makes you money and gives you a great return on investment. A *website* hardly ever makes money for the business owner. Most websites just kind of sit there and don't do much of anything.

As you can undoubtedly see from only five examples, a comprehensive, workhorse website is a much different marketing tool than just a simple, regular website. It is not a few paragraphs and some bullet points It is the complete story, solid case and proof of why a prospect should hire you.

A comprehensive, workhorse website allows prospects to get to know you in a non-threatening environment. They can read about your services, how you work with your clients, the results you get for your clients, your expertise and why you are the right person to hire, plus much, much more, without the fear of being "sold." They can explore and get to know you first, warm up to you and then be motivated to pick up the phone and call you.

There are so many things you can do with your comprehensive, workhorse website, the possibilities are almost endless. You can build a complete case for your expertise and services. You can write and post articles on your website so that your prospects see how you can solve various problems they face. You can visually show a prospect the results you can achieve for them with pictures, video, illustrations, etc. You can have complete descriptions of the services you provide to your clients. You can have convincing testimonials and case studies from your current and past clients, and on and on.

Minimum Comprehensive, Workhorse Website™ Sections

Here's a listing and explanation of the bare minimum sections you must have in a comprehensive, workhorse website. Within each of these sections, you need to build an entire case and story for the section. For example, on the Services page, don't just list all of the services you provide—list the services, explain each one in detail, explain how they will solve the prospects' pain, problem or predicament and why the prospect should hire you for this service.

Home Page

Don't even think of putting "welcome to my website" on your home page. If you have already done so, do not pass go, do not collect $200. The home page is a place to grab prospects' attention immediately, or they're gone. Start with the prospects. Talk about them, their pain, problem or predicament, and give them a snapshot of how you understand and how you can help. The home page must draw prospects in and move them to look at the other sections of your website.

Who We Work With

Write a complete description of the types of clients you have and work with, what their values are and what their goals and personalities are like. Explain who is a good fit to work with you and who isn't. Explain what types of jobs or industries your clients are involved in, etc. The more detail about what your clients "look like," the better. Paint a visual picture in the mind of your prospect so they can see themselves and know if they are a good fit or not. You can also have a client list in this section.

How We Work

Explain in detail how you work with your clients. Discuss all of the steps and/or processes you use with each client. Be specific, list the first, second, third and other steps. Give stories and illustrations, if possible.

Portfolio (Samples of Work)

This section will probably only apply if you are in the arts, architecture, photography or design profession. But, it is also a section that should be included by solo small businesses such as cosmetic dentists, cosmetic surgeons or remodelers and contractors. Basically, if your solo small business is one where a prospect can see a visual representation of what you do, then a visual showing of your work on your comprehensive, workhorse website is *not* optional. Remember to include as wide a variety as possible of the best samples of your work.

Services

This section is a comprehensive listing and explanation of every single service you provide to your clients and all the benefits they will receive from working with you, as I mentioned earlier. Remember, comprehensive means comprehensive … no bullet points or a few sentences. Explain your services in detail.

Why Choose Us?

Build a complete case explaining why someone should choose you over your competition. Remember to focus on the prospects first—what's in it for them, what they get, etc.—and you last. Give them every possible reason why you are the right one to hire. You must dig deeper than just your years of experience or how great your customer service is—everyone says that and it has come to mean very little. Give your prospects more compelling reasons.

Testimonials

Include as many testimonials from current and past clients as possible. Use full names plus city, state, business name and job title, if possible, in testimonials. This makes them much more credible. We'll go into more detail on testimonials in a later chapter.

About Us

Now it's time to toot your horn. This section is all about you, your background, your training, your expertise and your years in business. You can also toot your business' horn, if it has a track record. Also describe the skills and experience of your employees, if you have any.

Contact Page

List every possible way to get in contact with you: phone, fax, email, mailing address, physical address, 800 number, office hours, office location, office map and directions. In a comprehensive, workhorse website, there should be a Contact page, but, if possible, also list as much of this information as you possibly can at the bottom of every page of your site. Make it easy for clients to contact you.

Again, these are *bare minimum* sections you need in your comprehensive, workhorse website. If you don't include at least these minimum sections, you have just a website, not a comprehensive, workhorse one.

Additional Comprehensive, Workhorse Website™ Sections

Other sections I *highly recommend* you include, in addition to the bare minimum sections listed above are:

Free Stuff and eZine Sign-up

Capturing your prospects' email addresses when they visit your website is essential. Once you have a prospect's email address, you can market to them again and again. A great way to continually market to your prospects, even after they have left your website, is with a newsletter that's delivered via email (called an eZine). In order to capture visitors' email addresses, it's usually mandatory to offer them something for free. You can offer your prospects a free article, report or something else of value in exchange for their email address and signing up for your eZine. I recommend that you have a Free Stuff page on your site. On that page, have a sign-up form and explanation of the free stuff they will get once they give you their email address. Require visitors to give you their email address before you give them something for free.

Case Studies

Use case studies to illustrate the before-and-after results you have achieved for clients and give prospects a snapshot showing how you can help them, as well. I explain how to develop an effective case study later in this chapter.

Articles

Highlight your expertise in an area by providing prospects with valuable information they can use now in the form of articles or even a special report. I explain how to develop effective articles later in this chapter.

Client List

This is simply a listing of your clients, their business names and industries. It's more effective if you have clients at companies that are well known versus small local businesses. Saying you've done work for Wells Fargo®, Apple®, Nike® and Best Buy® is very impressive to your prospects and can "seal the deal" for those looking to work with solo small businesses that have worked with the big guys. Even if your clients are smaller and not readily known, you should still list the business name and industry. This will give prospects a feel for the types of businesses you work with.

Expected Results

This is a powerful explanation of what prospects can expect when they hire you. If it works in your world, you may even offer a guarantee. Most people think that guarantees are only for products (your battery is guaranteed for the life of your car), but solo small business owners who sell a service can (and should) offer guarantees to their clients, as well.

Resources

This is a list of links to other sites, articles or organizations of interest, or items that might help your prospect and provide more value from their visit. Essentially, you can become a source for information and a clearing house of helpful resources. Be careful that you do not have so many links to other websites that all of your visitors leave to go other places.

Forms and Download Area

If your solo small business requires forms, questionnaires or contracts for clients to begin working with you, your comprehensive, workhorse website is a great place to have them available for download. A prospect can visit this section of your site, download a form, fill it out and bring it to the appointment, thereby saving them time and shortening the sales cycle for you.

Schedule of Events

If one of your three to six strategically diversified marketing tools or activities is speaking or giving workshops, it is a good idea to list a schedule of upcoming events on your website. You can even take it one step further and have online registration to your events or have prospects sign up to receive a schedule or announcement of an event via email.

News, Awards and Announcements

If you score that big new client or win that prestigious award, tell people about it on your site. Remember, people learn and make decisions in many different ways. For some prospects, awards are very important. I have had clients hire me simply because of the awards I have won for my graphic design, website design and marketing work. You can also post press releases or news about your business. If you choose to post news on your site, it may or may not be solely about your business. You can post industry news or news that you know will affect your prospects in some way. You can make special announcements of special offers or other announcements that would be valuable to your prospects.

The Case for the Comprehensive, Workhorse Website™

As you can see, there is so much that a comprehensive, workhorse website can do to help you market your business. It's a shame that so many solo small businesses don't take full advantage of this incredibly powerful marketing tool.

Compared to other marketing tools and activities, a comprehensive, workhorse website is one of the most cost-effective and best uses of your solo small business marketing dollar.

When you develop a comprehensive, workhorse website, the up-front cost will be the greatest. You will have to pay for writing, layout and design, programming, testing and hosting. But the cost to operate your site over the years is very inexpensive. Basically, you will only continue to pay for hosting and your domain name (for example: www.yourwebsite.com), regular updates and additions (unless, of course, you do it yourself) and perhaps, an occasional small tweak or update to your website's look.

Bottom line: A comprehensive, workhorse website is a tool that your solo small business can't afford to be without.

Direct Mail

Direct mail is a relatively inexpensive and very effective means for a small business to attract clients on a consistent basis. Most small business owners hear "direct mail" and think, "That's junk mail." Let's look at the difference.

Direct Mail or Junk? What's the Difference?

In its simplest definition, direct mail is specifically targeted mail with a specific offer sent to a specific person who matches a specific profile. Junk mail is just ... junk. It is sent to a huge, nonspecific list with no target market in mind and speaks in generalities that will, theoretically, appeal to the greatest number of people. Large corporations can afford to paper an entire city with a junk mail campaign. As a solo small business owner, you can't. Unfortunately, many solo small businesses think they are sending out direct mail, when in reality it's junk.

Direct mail hits a prospect right where it "hurts"—the pain, problem or predicament. It talks directly to the prospects and focuses directly on them first and you second. It is mailed to a specific target (your niche) and not to the mass of humanity. Direct mail initiates a response, gets action and motivates prospects to do something now versus later. Bottom line: Direct mail works. Junk mail doesn't.

The Key Elements of Successful Direct Mail

There are five key elements that make a direct mail campaign successful. If any one of these five elements is missing, it's not direct mail. It's junk mail and will not be a successful campaign or good use of your money.

The next time you get an itch to send out a little postcard, or flyer or sales letter for your small business, stop. Do not lick the stamp or seal the envelope until you make sure that you have all five key elements in place for your mailing.

The 5 key elements in successful direct mail are:
1. The list

Your mailing list is the *most* important element in direct mail success. Bad list = bad results. The best list you can use is your house list: the list of clients and prospects that you know and who know you. If you have to purchase a cold list, there are a couple of things to keep in mind:

➤ Purchase lists from a reputable vendor or list broker, not the cheapest company you can find. There's a list of reputable mailing list brokers in the Appendix.

➤ Don't just buy a list of people or businesses in a five-mile radius of your business; go a few steps deeper. What is the income level of the clients you want to attract? What are their interests? Have they bought or had an interest in your type of services in the past? The more details you can come up with, the better the list will be.

Details are key to a useful mailing list. Too many small businesses just settle for a generic list such as families in a five-mile radius of their location or new small business owners, without any other identifiers at all. You need to get as specific as possible with the type of prospects you are looking for and then find that list. List companies and brokers can help you. When you approach them, say, "Here is a list of 25 characteristics of my prospects. What list can I buy that closely matches these criteria?" It's their job to help you find the perfect list.

2. The offer

Your offer is the second most important element. Too many mailings solo small business owners send offer nothing, zip, nada. Don't make this mistake. You must have an offer. And don't wimp out here—make your offer irresistible. It can be an offer for a free special report, a free trial, a free gift, a free consultation, etc. Offer something of value in your campaign. The offer is what makes the prospect perk up and take action. If your offer is weak, your results will be weak.

3. The copy

Copy is next. If you have a great offer and a great list, but don't communicate in a way that inspires clients to respond, your campaign will bomb. On the other hand, you can write the most perfect copy ever, but if you have the wrong list or a bad offer, it won't fly. It doesn't matter if angels sing when reading your copy; if it's describing a bad offer to a bad list, no one will buy.

4. The frequency

Frequency is a fancy term for the number of times you actually mail the piece. Most solo small businesses grossly underestimate just how many times prospects need to see a message before they decide whether or not to act. So what do you think? Three times, five times, seven times? How many times do you think a prospect needs to see a message before they actually start to "get it" and are ready to make a decision to buy? There are a lot of different numbers floating around out there, but most marketing research and industry experts will say that a person must see a message at least nine times before he makes a purchase decision.[3] That's *nine times ... nine with an 'n'*. And today, with most prospects having an attention span of a gnat, it can take a whole lot more. So, how many times did you send out your last mailing before you gave up?

---

3 *Small Business Advertising Basics* (www.AllBusiness.com). Ernest Nicastro, *How to Win Over the Man in the Chair: Salesmanship, Repetition and Direct Mail* (www.MarketingProfs.com: March 22, 2005). *Guerrilla Marketing for the New Millennium* (www.GuerrillaMarketingAssociation.com) Chapter 5.

5. The design

This is hard for me to say, being a graphic designer and all, but the design of your mailing piece is last. It's the least important of the five elements of success. Please don't think that just because design is last means you can send out something that looks horrible. Your direct mail piece needs to look professional, or people won't take you seriously. But, you have four other very important items to focus on first. Make sure they are in place and then focus on and perfect the design.

The Postcard as a Direct Mail Piece?

Many direct mail mavens follow a strict—and somewhat expensive—formula for direct mail that includes a two-page or longer sales letter, a brochure, a reply card, all in an envelope. There might even be another envelope in there for the reply card.

Now, don't get me wrong … this kind of direct mail piece works very well—I have used it myself and for my clients with great success; but it has drawbacks. It can be very expensive to write, design, produce and mail. It takes a lot of skill and study to write an effective two-plus-page direct mail letter—a skill that most solo small business owners don't possess or have the money to hire someone who does have the skill.

Luckily, there's a very effective and less expensive option: the postcard. A postcard is much easier to write and design. It's compact, yet has enough room for your message—it's short, sweet and to the point. It also cuts out the step where your prospect has to decide whether or not to tear into an envelope to see your message.

Postcards are easy to create, easy to mail and hold up very well to post office handling and delivery. I use direct mail postcards almost exclusively for my solo small business and my private clients' small businesses as well. I suggest that you do the same.

True, a postcard can't convey all the information that the standard two-plus-page direct mail letter and brochure can—it isn't meant to. The purpose of a direct mail postcard is to give your prospect a quick and focused message that will pique their interest and move them closer to finding out more about you.

One thing though ... I am not a fan of a standard 4.5" x 6" postcard. They're just too small. They get lost in a pile of mail, and there's not enough room on them to develop a good message and offer. The postcard size I swear by is the half-size, meaning half of an 8.5" x 11" sheet of card stock, or 5.5" x 8.5". Some vendors produce 6" x 9" or 6.5" x 8.5" cards, which is basically their half-size card. I highly recommend you use this size in your postcards and stay away from the tiny guys. The half-size cards do cost more to mail, requiring a full first class stamp, but there's no envelope, which is a big savings.

Final Thoughts on Direct Mail

Keep these things in mind when thinking about or planning your direct mail campaign:

Once is NEVER enough.

Don't take the "I'll just mail this out once and see what happens" approach. Don't even think about it. If that's your attitude, then don't waste your money. You need to approach direct mail as a series of mailings over a period of time. If you can't afford to design, print and mail at the bare minimum of six times, then forget it. You'll be wasting time and money. Choose another marketing activity.

In Chapter 12, I'll talk about what I call *lather, rinse and repeat*. Prospects have to see your message over and over and over and over again before they even begin to make a decision. Again, marketing research has concluded that a prospect must see a message nine times before they get it. You can't just mail out something once or twice or three or four times and expect results. It simply won't work.

Mailing six times is the BARE minimum, mailing twelve times is even better.

If you have the budget to design, print and mail something once a month—to the same list of prospects—for an entire year, results will follow. I have seen this time and time again. If your budget doesn't allow this, the bare minimum is six times (at least once a month) to the same list.

Not sure what to offer? Ask your previous clients.

Ask your clients what would attract them to your business. What would they like a deal on? What would convince them to pick up the phone and call? Ask and then act. Make the offer irresistible. If it wouldn't move you or your existing clients to find out more, then keep working on the offer.

Direct Mail Works!

I am a big fan of direct mail postcards. It is my vehicle of choice for my small business and many of my private clients. But whatever direct mail vehicle you decide to use—postcards, letters, flyers, etc.—just do it. Direct mail *is* a great tool to use as a solo small business, when your small business is you. For a list of recommended resources for your direct mail campaigns, see the Appendix.

Networking

I've talked about active versus passive marketing, as well as the absolute need to get out there and be visible to prospective clients. One of the best active, visible marketing activities is networking. Networking events include parties, mixers, luncheons, group meetings, business after-hours, get-togethers, etc.

No matter the size of the town or city where you live (unless of course you live in a teeny-tiny town, which probably isn't the best place to run a small, service-based business), there should be at least one Chamber of Commerce, more likely, a few of them. Chambers are a great way to network with other small business owners. Most Chambers hold networking events monthly or quarterly.

There are also a plethora of other networking and small business groups. Service clubs, such as Rotary International, Lions Club International and Kiwanis Clubs, are great for networking. So are professional and industry-specific organizations, and many, many other types of clubs and organizations. Check the business section of your local paper, or do a Google or Yahoo search for networking groups, and you will see a very long list of possibilities.

Attend, bring a stack of business cards and rub elbows with other small business owners who can be a resource for new business for you. This is part of being visible. No one can give you business unless they know you are in business.

Testimonials

Testimonials are a must when you're a solo small business owner! The minute you open your doors for business, you should be collecting testimonials from your clients. Testimonials are very, very powerful marketing tools. Many prospects will not do business with you unless you have a number of compelling and convincing testimonials from satisfied clients.

You need a testimonials section in your comprehensive, workhorse website. You also need testimonials in every other marketing tool you use and activity you participate in. You need to have testimonials on your brochures, collateral materials, website, direct mail campaigns, articles, case studies and your eZine or newsletter. In fact, I counsel my clients to have a testimonial sheet, a multi-page 8.5" x 11" packet of testimonials that they can give out to prospects. I have even seen some small business owners develop a testimonial diary. They actually buy a nice, leatherbound journal and have everyone of their clients write a handwritten message in the journal. When they meet with prospective clients, they have them flip through the journal to read praises from past clients. This is very effective.

Collecting Testimonials

When you ask for and collect testimonials, there are a few things you need to do:

Ask for specific details*.

Get numbers, statistics and figures, the more specific the better. This makes your testimonial much more powerful. For example: A testimonial that says, "Jeanna increased my business by $50,000 in one month" is much more powerful than, "Jeanna increased my business." Or, "By working with Jeanna, my client load will at least triple in the next four months" versus, "Jeanna will help increase my client load." See the difference specifics can make?

Use full names, city and state.

A testimonial signed: Tim Hamilton, Denver, Colorado is much more believable than a testimonial that's signed T.H. or T.H., Colorado. And, if you include the name of the business and the business title, all the better, such as Tim Hamilton, TH Construction, LLC, Residential Remodeling, Denver, Colorado. See how much more believable that is?

---

*Recently the FTC updated their guidelines for the use of testimonials. Be sure to visit: http://www.ftc.gov/opa/2009/10/endortest.shtm for more information and to make sure you are in compliance.

Get a testimonial from every single client you possibly can.

It is much better and easier to ask for a testimonial right after you finish working with a client. If the client does not know what to say, it's okay and completely ethical to offer to write the testimonial for them, then have them proof and tweak it so that it is in their words. I have done this with a few of my clients and often they'll say, "This looks great; I couldn't have said it better myself."

Use testimonials in every manner possible.

Remember, as a solo small business, you are selling yourself as the provider of the services you offer. Testimonials help you sell yourself better than almost any other tool you can use, so use them anywhere and everywhere you can.

One very successful way that I and some of my clients have used testimonials is to have a "call my clients" handout. This is where you pick two, four, or more past clients and get their permission for prospects to call them. Then list their full names, business names and phone numbers on a sheet that you can hand out. Give this to your prospects—essentially you are giving them permission to call these past clients and "grill" them about you. They can ask any question they want, and you encourage them to do so. This has proven very powerful and helped convince prospects that you really are who and what you claim to be.

Writing Articles

You may be thinking to yourself, "Writing articles? I'm not a writer. I'm a real estate agent. I don't know how to write!" I'm here to tell you, you don't have to be a writer to write effective articles to market your solo small business. All you have to do is write about what you know—and believe it or not, you know a lot!

You can hire a copywriter or editor to help polish your writing to make it more effective, but every single small business owner can and should use writing articles as one of their marketing tools.

Why Write Articles?

There are many, many, many reasons to write articles to market your solo small business. Here are just a few:

➤ Writing positions you as an expert in your field. Essentially, you're showing prospects that you are an expert on the topic you write about.

➤ Writing helps establish your credibility as the right solo small business to hire.

➤ Writing helps prospects get to know you and warm up to you; they get to know you through your writing.

➤ Prospects are inherently skeptical; writing helps prove to them that you *really do* know what you're talking about.

➤ Writing an article is a non-threatening way to promote your services. An article isn't an ad or a commercial or a sales piece. An article is information, and information is a great *stealth* type of marketing.

➤ Articles are a marketing method that focuses on the prospects first (and as you no doubt know by now, that's a great thing), because you are providing them with valuable information that they can use right now. It will benefit them and, as a natural progression, be drawn back to you.

➤ Writing articles can generate traffic—in most cases, a lot of traffic to your solo small business and comprehensive, workhorse website. When your article is listed on a third-party website or printed in a publication,

it always includes a credit line. That credit line can in
clude your contact information, a call to action and your
website address.

➤ Prospects trust articles more than advertisements. Think
about it: which do you put your trust in while reading
the newspaper or a magazine—the articles or the advertisements?

➤ Writing articles is inexpensive and cost effective. It can
cost no more than the paper it is printed on and if you
publish your article on the Internet, the cost to develop
the article is simply the time it takes to write it.

➤ Writing helps increase your own knowledge base and
clarify the way you speak about your industry. When you
write you learn and therefore know more about your own
subject matter. Writing what you know solidifies what
you know!

You can see that there are a lot of positive reasons to write articles
to market your solo small business. Now the question is, what types
of articles will you write? See the Appendix for more recommended
resources and help for writing articles.

Write Articles to Solve Problems

First and foremost with writing articles, the goal and focus is to
provide good information that will be helpful to your prospects. It all
goes back to the give-to-receive mentality. Prospects will be drawn to
you via your articles if they get information that will help them, not
sell them.

With that in mind, it's best to write articles from a helping, prob-
lem-solving and informational mindset. Simply think about the problems you can solve. What would prospects like to know about? What

are their questions? What information do you know that can help them? These are the topics to write about. Kind of sounds like the 3P approach, doesn't it? That's exactly what you want to focus on.

Now, I know what you're thinking, "Jeanna, as I said before, I am *not* a writer." If you think you're not a writer, just ask yourself: Do you know anything or have any information about your industry that could help potential prospects? Undoubtedly yes, right?! So write about it. Say you're in the real estate industry. You could write an article on "10 Ways to Sell Your House Fast in a Down Market," or "7 Pitfalls to Avoid When Buying a Home Built Before 1950." Notice that these articles are from a helping, not selling, perspective. And, more than likely, a pain, problem or predicament wrapped up in those topics. The fact that you write about pertinent subjects and give prospects good information sells you and your expertise.

Successful Formulas for Article Topics

There are many types of articles you can write. The good news is that you don't have to get fancy or experiment too much, because there are a few proven formulas that work very well. You've no doubt seen and read articles like this; you've seen them and read them because they work! The proven types of articles you should focus on are:

How-to articles

For example: "How to Save Money on Taxes," "How to Draft a Perfect Proposal," "How to Lose 10 Pounds in 10 Days," etc. Simply pick a topic and write "how-to" succeed, accomplish, or do the subject of your article.

Number-of-ways or number-of-steps articles

For example: "Seven Steps to a Flawless Golf Swing," "13 Ways to Save More Money," "Nine Ways to Close More

Business," etc. This type of article is my favorite to write and the most popular. You simply break-down your subject into steps or ways.

Do-You-Make-These-Mistakes articles

For example: "Do You Make These Mistakes in Your Business?," "Do You Make These Mistakes on Your Taxes?," etc. You can also combine this topic with the number-of-ways topic, such as, "Do You Make These 15 Mistakes in Your Sales Presentations?"

How-NOT-to articles

For example: "How NOT to Attract Clients Consistently," "How NOT to Buy an Investment Property," "How NOT to Shop for Auto Insurance," etc.

Fun-Titled articles

For example: "What the Three Little Pigs Can Teach Us About Running a Business," "Everything I Learned About Investing, I Learned from My Six-Year-Old Daughter," etc.

These are by no means the only article topics you can write, but it's a good list to get you started. Once you decide on the subject matter of your article, simply write what you know. Remember to keep it very informative. It needs to be loaded with practical advice—it's an article, not a direct sales pitch for your services.

Your articles don't have to be novels. Anywhere between 500 and 1,000 words is perfect. Give your prospects enough information to help them, but don't try to teach them everything in one fell swoop. Articles can be short and sweet while still being very effective.

Writing articles is a highly successful tool and activity to attract clients consistently. Many of my clients found me and decided to hire me based on the information I provided and taught them in the articles I have written and continue to write. Articles are definitely one marketing tool you should use as a solo small business owner.

eZine or Newsletter

After writing articles, the next logical and obvious tool is to produce an eZine or newsletter. An eZine is simply a newsletter that is written and delivered via email.

You can produce whichever format suits you best: eZine or a traditional, printed newsletter. Both are very effective. An eZine is much cheaper to produce. All you will need is a comprehensive Website where prospects can sign up to receive the eZine and a software solution to deliver the eZine to your email addresses. You must buy or subscribe to an eZine software solution—simply using your email program to send out the emails to subscribers will not work for very large lists or even lists of a few dozen subscribers. Most Internet service providers will mark an email with a long list of email addresses as spam. An eZine software solution will prevent this from happening. For a list of recommended eZine software providers and resources, see the Appendix.

A traditionally printed newsletter costs more to produce due to the printing and mailing costs; however, a traditionally printed newsletter is nice because your recipients actually have something to hold, flip through and keep, versus just another email. Both are very effective. The choice is usually a matter of budget and time available to devote to the tool.

How Often Should You Send an eZine or Newsletter?

Many solo small business owners think sending out a quarterly newsletter is enough. I completely disagree. Four times a year is nowhere near enough repetition and consistency to be worth the effort and expense of printing and mailing.

If you will be using an eZine or traditional newsletter as one of your three to six strategically diversified marketing tools, you need to send it out, at the bare minimum, once a month. If you can't do that, don't choose this as one of your tools. You can send your eZine or newsletter more times if you choose, but once a month is minimum.

Obviously, preparing an eZine this frequently is easier to manage than a traditional newsletter because of printing and mailing costs and transit times to get to your prospects. That's why eZines are so popular. I know some small business owners who send out their eZine twice a month, or even every single week. If you have the time to dedicate to this frequency while still maintaining good, solid, valuable content, then by all means do it. It certainly won't hurt for prospects to see your information more than once a month. They will really get to know you.

What to Include In an eZine or Newsletter

Your eZine or newsletter should, like the articles you write, be approached from the giving mentality. Give good information that helps people. Yes, you absolutely can and should have a sales pitch about your services in your eZine or newsletter, but the majority of the content should focus on information that will help your subscribers. A good rule of thumb is 70-30, meaning 70% of your eZine or newsletter is helpful information and no more than 30% is sales related. Some small business owners prefer an 80-20 approach; 80% information, 20% sales. That's what my monthly eZine is. Bottom line, however you split up the eZine or newsletter between information and sales, you should not have more than 30% dedicated to sales. If you do, people won't read it, because it will be just another sales pitch. The eZine for my solo small business is very effective, and I get a ton of comments from my readers about how much it helps them in their solo small businesses. I do sell my services in each issue, but again, my main focus is information. When you provide good, helpful, quality material, readers won't mind a small sales pitch.

Case Studies

Prospects usually don't just show up at your front door and say, "Let's get started!" Sure, I guess it could happen, but more times than not, a prospect needs a good reason to do business with you. So, what reason do you give your prospects? How do you convince prospects that you are the right person to work with?

A fantastic way to convert prospects into clients is to prove that you can help them. Prove that you are *the* expert to work with. Prove that you can and do get results. We all want results. We all want proof. One of the best ways to prove it and show results is the case study.

Why Case Studies?

A well-done case study proves to your prospect that you are indeed the expert to hire. Any solo small business owner can and should develop case studies for several reasons:

> ➤ Case studies are a very effective and non-threatening way to market the results that you can and have achieved with your clients.
> ➤ Case studies are very believable, because you're not selling yourself. You're telling a true story, and the results that you and your client have achieved are selling your services.
> ➤ Case studies are easy to create, and the only cost involved is the paper they're printed on.

Developing a Case Study

To develop a compelling case study for your services, follow these five steps:

Step 1: Choose the Case

Look over your client list. Choose three to five clients who have achieved outstanding results as a direct result of working with you. Choose businesses that have really benefited in a profound way. The bigger the results, the more proof you are giving your prospects that you are the right choice.

Step 2: Give the Background

The first section of a case study is the problem or background. What was the client's situation before you came onto the scene? What did he struggle with? What did he need fixed or changed? What was it that made him need or want to hire a business like yours?

Here's an example:

John Doe suffered from severe migraine headaches. Often his headaches were so painful that he had to take several days off from work and stay in bed. He had visited his doctor several times and was given a prescription to help with the pain, but the headaches just kept getting worse.

Step 3: Explain the Process Used

After the problem or background, the next section of a case study is the process. Spell out exactly what you did for the client to address and fix the problem you just described.

The first step in eradicating John's headaches was to perform a complete neurological physical examination. We also took a close look at John's diet, including everything he ate and drank, and investigated any possible allergies that may have been contributing to the problem. Lastly, we ran a thorough set of blood chemistry tests to check for any irregularities that might be triggering the migraines.

Step 4: Announce the Results

Results are the meat and potatoes of your case study. Don't hold back: spell out in detail exactly what the clients got, how things improved and how satisfied they were. If you have hard data or statistics, even better. This is the proof of the entire case study, so make sure it's compelling.

> Through John's blood chemistry and allergy testing, we discovered that he was allergic to certain fruit juices that he drank every morning, and that this allergy was the leading cause of his migraines. Many people do not realize that they have food allergies, and most of the traditional medical community fails to look for subtle allergies to help diagnose the root cause of problems like migraines.

> After a small change in John's diet and a two-week detox regimen, John's headaches disappeared. It has been over six months since he has suffered from a single migraine or even a mild headache. Had we not conducted our thorough blood chemistry and allergy testing on John, his migraines would have never been properly diagnosed.

Step 5: Call to Action

Wrap it up with a call to action. You have just told a story of a business or person with a problem or issue, what you did to solve it and what the results were. Now it's time to invite prospects to call you, so you can show them how you can achieve the same results for them.

> Do you suffer from debilitating migraines, as John did? Have you tried prescription medications with no results? If John's story sounds familiar, AAA Alternative Health Clinic can help. We have helped over 1,100 clients free their lives from migraines and other common health ailments. We get to the root cause of your problem, then eradicate it completely. And our services are a fraction of the cost of traditional medicine. Give us a call today for a complimentary consultation.

That's it! Those are the very simple, yet very powerful steps to developing a great case study. The example I used was for a fictional company, but you get the idea. The main thing to remember is to illustrate the story with powerful results. Powerful results are what really motivates a prospect to act.

Final Thoughts on Case Studies

A few things to remember about case studies are:

➤ If you have hard facts on the results you got for your clients, use them. "As a result of our work together, XYZ Client increased sales by 38% within a four-month period." That sounds more powerful than "XYZ Client increased their sales."

> If your client gives you a really good testimonial, use it in your case study right after the results section. Testimonials like "We love Lori; she is awesome and very fun to work with!" are great, but again, hard facts are better.

> You can never have too many case studies. I suggest that you write a case study for each separate issue or problem you've helped your clients with. For example, a chiropractor may have ten case studies ranging from low back pain to helping improve a golf swing. The more variety, the better. When prospects come to see you, you can give them a case study that parallels their issue or problem.

Develop case studies for your solo small business. They really are an easy, powerful, persuasive way to prove to your prospects that you really are the expert in your field.

Referrals and Referral Groups

Referrals are the number one way that solo small businesses build their client base. You probably depend on referrals for a good portion of your business, as well. So let me ask, do you actually have a system in place to generate referrals? Or do you just hope and pray that you do a good job, and the referrals will follow?

I recommend that all solo small business owners join a formal, structured referral organization. The organization I recommend is Business Network International, or BNI for short. See the Appendix for how to contact BNI.

Business Network International

I recommend BNI for one simple reason: it absolutely works. There are lots of leads groups and networking groups that you can get involved with: Chambers of Commerce, professional organizations, service organizations, industry-specific groups, etc., but, I've found BNI to be the most successful. I give BNI such a high recommendation for several reasons:

➤ First and foremost their purpose is to generate quality business word-of-mouth referrals for their members. Sure, members get to know each other and become friends, but business is first and socializing is secondary.

➤ Second, they have a strict attendance policy. If you've ever visited a casual leads group and found that you were the only person who showed up for the day (which I have), you will quickly appreciate how wonderful the attendance policy is. They make sure that their members are in attendance every week, so they experience the repetition of hearing about and learning about the other members' businesses. You can't refer to someone you don't know, and you can't get to know them if they are never in attendance.

➤ Third, they don't let just anyone join. You actually have to fill out an application, be interviewed and have references checked. Then they decide whether or not to accept you. This is important because when you recommend a professional to someone, it's your reputation on the line. If that professional isn't all he should be, you could end up looking stupid. Since BNI screens their potential members well, they sidestep the possibility of allowing someone into the group who is not really a good fit to refer business to. Membership in BNI is not automatic or permanent. If a member is accepted but turns out to be something other than what was first presented, that member can have his classification opened up for another professional to replace him.

➤ Lastly, BNI is a non-competing group, meaning they only allow one person per profession in each chapter. So, when you join BNI and you're a chiropractor, you will be the only chiropractor in the chapter. If you visit Chamber mixers, of course, there will be many people representing the same industry, so the competition is stiffer at Chamber functions than at BNI.

These are just four of many reasons why BNI is different and better than other networking groups. I have been involved in a BNI chapter for many, many years. In fact, I helped start the chapter I am involved with.

I recommend BNI to every one of my clients, and I recommend it to you, as well. I don't get paid or receive any type of compensation for recommending them. I do it because BNI works and it is one of the largest and most successful groups of its kind in the world.

If there isn't a BNI chapter near you, or if you visit and it is not a good fit for your small business, there are a lot of other referral groups you can join. The main thing is to join one! Some local Chambers of Commerce have dedicated referral groups you can join, in addition to the networking possibilities mentioned above.

Power Partners or Joint Ventures

I've borrowed a phrase often used in BNI, called *Power Partners*. Very simply, power partners are industries that are related in some way and are a natural fit for referring business to each other. Some examples are a printer and a graphic designer, a photographer and a wedding coordinator, a real estate agent and a mortgage broker, a CPA and a financial planner, an architect and an interior designer, etc. All solo small business owners should develop power partners.

Do some brainstorming to come up with a list of other industry professionals who would be a good fit to refer business to you and vice versa. It has to be a win-win situation. If you develop a relationship and you send them lots of business, but they don't reciprocate, you won't stay in that relationship very long, and vice versa. Once you have identified other industries, approach them and discuss the possibility of developing a relationship to give each other business when someone asks or the need arises. It's best if you develop relationships with a few different industries. And you may even want to work with two different businesses within one industry.

The goal of a power partner relationship is to build value now to earn money later. You become a more valuable resource for your clients. You also become a valuable resource for your power partners, which, in turn, eventually leads to more business between you. For example, I have power partner relationships with two printers. One is really good and priced competitively with smaller jobs. The other is really good and priced competitively with larger jobs and higher-end work. Whenever my clients need printing done, I am able to match them with the best printer for the job—the printer who will do the best work at the best possible price. This is a win-win for my clients and the printers, as well as for me, since the printers will be referring their customers to me when they need graphic design services.

Joint ventures are similar to power partner relationships, however, in a joint venture, both parties involved make money on every transaction or referral. For example, you may find a few industries to joint venture with to conduct a seminar. Everyone chips in for the cost and everyone splits the profits.

You can joint venture with someone to help you sell more of your services. For instance, a small business attorney could joint venture with a business coach. If the business coach sends clients to the attorney for contracts, setting up legal entities or other legal services, the coach gets a commission from the lawyer.

You can joint venture with someone so you can market to their client list. Let's say that I found a colleague who has a very large mailing list of prospects in a niche that I want to focus on. We could form a joint venture where I get to market to that list, with my colleague's recommendation. As compensation, I would pay my joint venture a percentage of the new business I get.

Joint ventures are a great way to speed up the sales process and quickly attract new clients. Like the power partner relationship, it is a win-win for everyone. You get clients, your joint venture gets a cut and the client gets his pain, problem or predicament solved.

I highly recommend you begin building both added value power partner relationships and money-making joint ventures for your solo small business.

Free Trials or Demos

Free trials or demos are fantastic tools and activities to market your services. Many small business owners use free trials in their marketing with very successful results. Life and business coaches offer free initial coaching sessions. Massage therapists offer free ten-minute massages. Free trails or demos let prospects get to know you, see how you work and essentially "try before they buy."

Think about all those free food samples you get when you visit the grocery store. Chances are, if you like the taste of the sample, you'll buy the product. You may not have been planning to buy it when you entered the store, but the sample worked and a sale was made. It's the same with your small business: free trials work. Skeptical prospects see exactly what they will be purchasing and know whether or not it's a fit for them.

A free initial consultation isn't necessarily an effective free trial or demo. If you give away a free initial consultation, you need to demonstrate how the prospects will benefit by working with you. Sitting down and discussing the prospects' pain, problem or predicament while trying to sign them up as a new client is not a free trial or demo. Discussing their 3Ps and working with them so they can see you in action—actually solving part of their problem, is. Demonstrate how you work, what they'll get and how they will benefit. The more you physically or visibly show them, the more effective your free trial or demo will be.

Promotional and Special Events

Why do real estate agents host open houses for their clients? Because it's a way to showcase a home and generate a lot of potential buyers in a short amount of time. You can do the same for your small business via promotional and special events.

A friend of mine, who is a very successful fine artist, holds special events all the time, with great success. She holds holiday art shows, spring art shows and "summer's gone" art shows, complete with snacks and drinks. She literally sells her paintings off of the wall. So, how can you achieve the same results for your service-based solo small business? Combine a free trial or demo with a promotional or special event.

You could hold a holiday open house. Invite clients and prospects to your office location, provide refreshments and give them a free trial of your services, or demonstrate how you work with clients. Have current and past clients talk about the results that they have achieved by working with you. Give a quick ten to thirty-minute informational session. Have a group discussion about a pain, problem or predicament and solve it for your attendees. With a little creative brainstorming, the possibilities are endless.

I heard a story about a fashion coordinator who held a "find your perfect clothing" event at an upscale boutique. She sent out invitations to her clients, inviting them to attend and bring one or two friends who did not know her, her service or how she worked. At the event, she demonstrated with a couple of her past clients how she works and exactly the results she achieves. She showed how she helps her clients find clothes that work with their hair, eyes and skin color, and perfectly fit their body shapes. She showed the "clothing cards" that she gives to clients to take along when they go shopping. She even combined this special event with a free demo—and also made a promotional offer for 10% off of her consulting package. She had a great number of attendees and signed up a handful of new clients. I'd say, that's not too bad for a few hours of work and a fun special event.

A previous client of mine is an independent representative of a large health food, vitamin and supplement company. She focuses on women's health and regularly holds special events to teach women about the benefits of a healthy diet and vitamins and supplements. She partners with other small businesses that help women with health-related or personal services. She always makes a lot of great contacts and generates a lot of new business from these events.

You, too, can benefit from special events. Partner with another business that complements your services. Develop a special event that incorporates the services you provide with a promotion just for attendees. Promotional and special events can be very successful activities to promote your solo small business.

Seminars, Workshops and Speaking

The last proven tool or activity for marketing your small business effectively as a solo, is conducting seminars, holding workshops or speaking to groups.

You've probably noticed that almost all of the tools and activities for marketing your solo small business focus on two things: one, helping and focusing on your prospects by providing them valuable information; and two, positioning yourself as the expert and authority in your field as the right choice for your prospects to hire. There's a reason for this ... it works!

No other tool or activity lets you showcase both your expertise and share valuable information with your prospects better than seminars, workshops and speaking engagements. This combination consistently attracts new clients. It does for my solo small business and it will for yours too.

Seminar or Workshop: What's the Difference?

Many people use the terms seminar and workshop interchangeably, but technically, there is a difference. A seminar is usually a single half-day or full-day teaching session on one subject. A workshop is usually a multi-day event. It may cover multiple subjects, or just one subject, but it is more in-depth than in a seminar. Workshops are sometimes seen as "hands-on" learning, while seminars are seen as "lecture" type learning. Speaking is just that—speaking to a group of people, usually on one subject, for thirty minutes to one hour or longer.

How To Pick a Topic

Picking a topic for a seminar, workshop or speaking engagement is like picking a topic for your articles. What do your prospects want to know? What do they want to learn about? What is the pain, problem or predicament they want solved? What have you heard your past and current clients complain about?

Brainstorm a list of topics using these questions, and you'll be surprised how many topics you'll come up with. Then it's simply a matter of teaching and talking about what you know.

Free or for a Fee?

You can do speaking engagements for free or for a fee. Unless you're a very good, well-known and sought-after speaker, chances are you won't be hired for a whole lot of paid speaking engagements. Don't let that stop you. Speak to a group for free. Speak to as many groups as possible for free. Provide the audience with a lot of great information, and you *will* get new clients. Plus, the more you speak, the better you'll become, and the more well known you'll be. And that may eventually lead to paid speaking engagements—just don't expect it from the get-go.

I counsel my clients to speak for free as often as they can. There is no cost involved, except for their time. Over half of the time that my clients speak for free, they get a new client as a result.

I generate a lot of business from speaking, plus, speaking is a lot of fun for me. I am not a shy person; in fact, I'm quite gregarious, so speaking is a very natural fit and an excellent tool that I use again and again.

Conducting seminars or workshops is another great tool; however, there is more cost involved, compared to speaking. At the bare minimum, you have the cost of advertising and marketing the event and securing a location. Then there's the cost of handouts, refreshments and audio/visual equipment rental.

I highly recommend that you do not conduct free seminars and workshops. Charge a fee for your seminars and workshops. Even if it is only $29, charge something.

People often don't take free seminars and workshops all that seriously. Many people see free seminars and workshops as glorified sales pitches. There are many industries that are notorious for this. It's a total bait-and-switch. They advertise a "free" informational seminar, but when you get there, there is very little information and a lot of sales pressure. Do *not* do this. People see right through it, and when prospects who really expect to learn something do attend, they feel used and taken advantage of, when it's just a big dog-and-pony show. It's a huge turn-off.

Seminars and workshops can be very effective. Again, you are helping your prospects out and showcasing your expertise at the same time. Just make sure that you provide a lot of really valuable content. People attend seminars and workshops to learn something. Don't disappoint them. Teach them all you can. They are paying you to teach them something. Make it more than worth the money they paid, and you will be successful.

What if You're Not Very Good at Speaking?

The more you speak, the better you will get. If you need help, there are several ways to get training. You can take a class in public speaking, read books on speaking, join a networking or referral group where you give talks about your services, or join a Toastmasters chapter; but there is simply no substitute for getting out there and speaking. Practice makes perfect. See the Appendix for recommended resources for conducting seminars and workshops and speaking engagements.

Social Media

Social media can be a great way to market your solo small business, but only if it's done the right way.

Social media can either be a great way to build relationships with prospective clients, add more subscribers to your eZine, build your online image and move prospects into paying clients … or it can be a huge time sucking vortex of wasted hours and wasted effort with little or no results from your efforts. The difference between the two is learning how to use social media the right way for marketing.

Social media really is a specialty all by itself. Entire books, seminars, conferences and bootcamps have been created on just this topic alone. So rather than try to tackle the huge subject of marketing via social media, I've listed the best resources for learning how to use social media the right way in the Appendix.

Video

Thanks to YouTube.com, video is usually considered a branch of social media, however there are so many fantastic ways to market your services with video, that it should not *only* be thought of as a part of social media.

Just like seminars, workshops and speaking, video is a great way to showcase both your expertise and share valuable information with your prospects. This is because prospects get to see you and know you when they watch your video.

There are literally dozens if not hundreds of ways you can market your solo small business successfully with video, here are just a few of my favorite that can be used both offline and online:

➤ Shoot a video welcome message to use on your comprehensive, workhorse website. In the video, you can direct visitors to sign up for your eZine or direct them to specific areas of your site.

➤ Take five or ten of the most common questions you get asked about your industry or services and shoot a video that answers each one*. This can be great free content to give to prospective clients.

➤ Take five or ten of the questions your prospective clients *should be asking* before working with someone in your

*I first learned of this Q&A and should be asking video marketing strategy from Mike Koenigs of Traffic Geyser, www.TrafficGeyser.com.

industry and shoot a video that answers each one*. For example: a remodeling company could create a video on "What is your Better Business Bureau rating and complaint status? A question you *should be asking* before hiring any remodeling company."

➤ Shoot a video and use it as a sales presentation or demo for your services. Here, the video becomes a powerful show-and-tell that demonstrates what prospective clients get when they hire you and all of the components your service entails. Using video this way can literally be as powerful as discussing your services live, face-to-face with prospects.

➤ Take your testimonials to a whole new level and shoot video testimonials. You can use these on your comprehensive, workhorse website or even create a DVD full of testimonials to give away to prospects. Imagine how powerful your testimonials will be when prospective clients can hear *and* see your clients in their own words!

➤ Create your own "online TV show." To do so, simply shoot videos that give tips, strategies, resources and other types of useful information for your prospective clients (the videos don't need to be very long, five to ten minutes is perfect). Then post the videos online on a consistent schedule, such as weekly, bi-weekly or monthly, and voila, you have your own "online TV show!" Who knows, you may even end up on a real TV show from your efforts! Gary Vaynerchuk has a great "online TV show" at www.WineLibrary.tv.

As you can see, video is very powerful marketing tool. The possibilities for using it to market your solo small business are limited only by your imagination.

Now, I know what you're thinking, "Jeanna I don't know anything about video, besides to shoot and edit video is expensive. I will have to buy an expensive camera or hire a videographer to help me. This is way out of my league." If that sounds familiar, good news … that is simply not the case!

First, your videos do not have to be Hollywood production quality. Low cost and even homemade looking video is just fine. The most important elements of video marketing success is giving good information in your video and that your personality shows through. Be yourself and help people. If you do these two things, you *will* succeed with video.

Second, all you need to get started is an inexpensive video camera and editing software. You can get many great video cameras for less than $200 and for editing software … iMovie comes installed on most Macs and is great! If you have a PC, simply search online for "cheap video editing software" and you'll find lots of options.

Of course you can go the route of hiring a professional videographer to do it all for you and buying the best and most expensive equipment out there. But, I recommend starting small and getting your feet wet. Then if you decide video marketing is for you (hint, hint, it should be, because it's super powerful) you can upgrade.

Press Releases

Press releases can be a very low cost and effective way to market your solo small business. Two great things about marketing with press releases is, first, they're a happy medium between strictly news and strictly promotion … they blend the two very successfully. Second, the only cost involved is the time it takes you to write and submit your press release and the fees charged if you use an online distribution service.

I have had great success marketing everything from my books to speaking engagements to seminars and bootcamps with press releases. They are a very powerful tool that works! If you are not marketing your services with press releases the time to start is now!

There's a lot of information available about press releases and PR in general, but the very best teacher on how to market a solo small business with press releases is my friend and colleague Marc Harty. Check out the Appendix for Marc's contact information and other recommended resources.

Final Thoughts on Choosing the RIGHT Tools and Activities

Remember in the last chapter we discussed strategic diversification (choosing between three and six marketing tools and activities to use in marketing your solo small business)? Now it's time to get busy. I've just listed a plethora of marketing tools and activities for you to choose from. These tools and activities are proven. These tools and activities work. Put them into practice, and you *will* enjoy success and get results for your solo small business. Dig in and choose your three to six.

Keep in mind that the three to six you choose to start with may or may not be the tools and activities you stay with. As you'll see in Chapter 11, it is imperative to test, test and test again. But, you can't test what you're doing until you dig in and actually start *doing*. ◆

Hiring Marketing Help

L et me ask you a question: How much money is your time worth? If you're like most solo small business owners, you make money *only* when you are working with your clients.

Do-It-Yourself or Hire an Expert?

You do *not* make money while you are answering email, driving the car, prospecting for clients and, above all, struggling to do things on your own that you're not qualified to do or have absolutely no business doing. You can't be an expert in everything.

It never ceases to amaze me how many solo small business owners burn up precious time—and money—doing things they have absolutely no business doing. Time is a precious gift. Once spent, you cannot get it back. When you're a solo small business, time *is* money. Yeah, you've heard that a million times, but do you really take it to heart? Do you spend your working day—your pay time, the daylight you have from 8AM to 5PM—making money or, at the very least, doing the things that *will* make you money? Or do you spend it on other things and activities that cost you money?

So, what does this have to do with marketing? Glad you asked. Bottom line, your time is expensive—very expensive. Whatever you charge your clients, that's how expensive your time is. Make sure that spending those expensive hours is really saving you money versus costing you. Do the math: if you charge $50, $75, $100, $300 per hour, doing things that you are not qualified to do will cost you, not save you.

Imagine for a moment that you are the CEO of a large corporation. Let's say you are the CEO of IBM®. Would you do the hiring for the company, or would you let HR do that? Would you do all of the sales for the company, or would you let your sales team do that? Would you do all of the accounting for the company, or would you let your CFO and accounting team do that? Would you design brochures and direct mail campaigns, or would you let the marketing department do that?

Imagine how crazy it would be for the CEO to do the hiring, sales, accounting and marketing for IBM. There is no way that would ever happen. IBM has departments of experts who focus on what they do best. And, therefore, IBM is a very successful company. The collaborative effort of the experts allows the company to make tons of money.

It's the same with your business. Your small business is you. You are the CEO, yet most solo small business CEO's do everything themselves. It's no wonder why so many solo small businesses struggle to make ends meet. It's no wonder why so many small businesses struggle to attract clients consistently. It's no wonder why solo small businesses simply struggle.

How can you be profitable when you spread yourself so thin by doing everything yourself? This is and always will be a very expensive waste of your time. The most profitable companies, large or small, are those that know when to farm out the tasks to the experts. Want to make more money? Want to be more successful? Want to attract a consistent client load? Then focus first on what you do best and hire out the rest.

This is another area in which you need to change your thinking: doing everything yourself does not save time and money. The sooner you come to this realization, the better. Imagine having all of your time dedicated to what you do best and what makes you the most money. Hiring help frees up your time and makes you more money.

Even the Lone Ranger had Tonto. Get help!

The Case for Hiring a Professional

There are a number of different services that the successful solo small business owner hires for help. Since this book is about marketing, we'll focus on the who and how-to of hiring help with an aspect of your small business' marketing, primarily, a designer.

How Much Should I Spend? And Why Should I Spend Any Money at All?

A professional, consistent image and marketing materials that actually work to sell you and get you clients are vital to your company's success. Too many solo small business owners make the mistake of hiring the cheapest designer they can find to design their logo, stationery, brochures, website, etc., or they try to design these items themselves.

Unless you're an expert in design with a degree and years of experience, stick to working at the business you know, and leave the design work to the designers. What you have to realize is that you only pay the cost to design your logo, stationery, brochure, website and other identity materials *once*—once that is, with money—but you'll pay for them again and again, each and every single time someone sees them. If your materials project a professional, consistent image, then that transaction pays you in good will, trust and future business. If the image is amateurish or inconsistent, then you lose trust, confidence and money.

I see this every day and it makes me want to pull my hair out: small business owners who buy $99 logos on the Internet, or get their best-friend's-boyfriend's-brother's-girlfriend to design their logo because she just got a new computer and is a little "artsy."

You *will* pay for this. Oh, yeah, just $99 bucks now. But every single time someone sees that logo, you'll pay and pay and pay and pay. I know you're on a budget. I know money is tight. I hear it all the time. It's the same for just about every small business owner—we don't have venture capitalists and shareholders to bankroll us—but, the thing you must realize is, hiring a professional designer is an investment you *must* make. Your professional image and long-term success depend on it. If you're serious about being in business, you can't afford *not* to hire a professional. Period.

You may think hiring a designer who charges $1,000 for a logo or $5,000 to $10,000 for a website design is steep, but you have to think about this: if you hire a really fantastic professional who really knows what she's doing and has an outstanding portfolio, you will only pay that fee once. And you'll reap the financial rewards of having a professional image and design that sells for years to come. If you go for the low-priced amateur design, not only will you not project an image that will move prospects to trust and hire you, chances are you'll also end up paying someone else in the future to redesign your image to get you the results you desire.

I once sat across the desk from a prospect who was interested in having me redesign the website for his business that he designed himself years ago. He told me he wanted his website to be a comprehensive, workhorse website that I teach about (give him points for realizing he needed a professional to design and create his website). He told me that he was looking at me and one other designer. He had already seen the other designer and gotten a quote from him.

We spoke, and I quoted him my fee to design redesign his comprehensive, workhorse website. He said, "I really like your portfolio better than the other designer and I know you are an expert at marketing, but your fee is about five times the other designer's fee."

I graciously explained that when he works with me, he will only have to pay my fee once and never pay for his website again, and that the comprehensive, workhorse websites I create for my private clients actually sell and make money! But, he decided to go with the other designer. Which is fine. That's his choice. I'm not a fit for everyone.

About two months later, I got a call from him. "Jeanna, could you come back to my office? I would like to hire you to design my website." When I got to his office, I asked, "What happened?" He said, "Well, you were right. I hired the other designer, and after two months I could see that I made a mistake. Yeah, he was a lot cheaper than you were, but I this is not the type of website I need. I need a site that sells. This isn't any better than the one I originally designed. So now it's time to hire you."

I thanked him, and over the next few months, I designed his comprehensive, workhorse website. Just two weeks after the new site was launched he got a client via the website, worth several million dollars to his business. Now I can't say that you will make millions when you hire outside help. But, the moral of the story: spend the money to do things right the first time and hire the right professionals and experts to help you. He ended up paying the other designer's fee and my fee, but that's it. He never had to pay again. If he had stayed with designer number one, he would have paid his fee and continued to paid every single day after that because his website would not have been an effective marketing tool.

Finding the RIGHT Graphic Designer & Website Designer

Hiring the right graphic designer or website designer—a true expert and professional—whether for printed materials or for a website, is a bit more involved than randomly choosing someone from the Yellow Pages or hiring your third cousin because he is creative and owns a new computer. When you look for a designer, there are a few things to keep in mind:

Professional Design is an Investment, NOT an Expense

You need to be willing to invest in hiring a qualified, experienced professional. Don't hire the cheapest person you can find. The old adage is true: you get what you pay for. Naturally, your budget is an important issue in choosing a designer. But, if you shop on price alone, I promise you will get exactly what you pay for. Stay away from the $29, $49, $99 or, heaven forbid, free "logo designers" you see on the Internet. 99% of those so-called designers are people with a computer, some fonts and cutesy clip art. They are not professional designers. Oh sure, they'll say they are, but real professionals value their craft and never want to be the cheapest—which is exactly what most of these "designers" are. The same goes for website design. Stay away from cheap templates and free website graphics if you want your image to convey the professionalism you desire.

Not All Designers Are Created Equal

Just because someone says that they're a designer doesn't mean that the person is necessarily worth their salt. The key here is to examine that person's portfolio of work. Effective design is more than pretty pictures or cool graphics. It is a visual means of solving complex business problems by communicating the essence of your business message and personality. Therefore, when you are looking at the designer's portfolio, don't just take a quick look. Dig in and ask many questions about the work. What was the design problem? How was it solved? What was the concept behind the design solution? Why were those colors chosen? Why was that format chosen? What were the results? Was the client satisfied? If the designer can't answer these questions or answers with "I did it this way because it looks cool," or "I used yellow because it's my favorite color," run away as fast as you can.

Check References

If the designer you are considering has done a stellar job for previous and/or current clients, that professional should not hesitate to give you names of people who will attest to that fact. Giving no references should be taken as a big red flag. When contacting references—and you should—ask questions about the overall experience with the designer. Is the designer a professional? Would you use the designer again? Do you feel you got your money's worth? Did he or she deliver the project within the agreed upon time frame and budget? Does the finished piece solve your problem? Ask as many questions as you think apply to your particular situation.

Honestly Discuss Your Budget

Budget is the proverbial 800-pound gorilla in the middle of the room. Everyone has a budget in mind, but not many want to discuss it. If you have done steps one through four, you will be close to hiring someone who is not a trained sales killer and is not just interested in taking all of your money, so you can be open and honest with them. Having a candid discussion with the designer about what you can practically afford is vital, for a few reasons.

➤ First, it lets both of you know, right off the bat, whether you can work together. You won't waste time wondering, "How much is this really going to cost me?" or "Do I have the money to hire this person?"

➤ Second, it will allow for a discussion of what you can expect in exchange for the money you will spend. Obviously, the key is to hire a designer who can work within your budget. To do that, you *must* have an honest and open discussion about money. No one wants a last-minute surprise about what it will cost to work together.

One Last Thing About Hiring A Designer ...

You should view the graphic designer or website designer you hire as your strategic business partner and a valuable member of your team. Sure, you can hire a pro just once to create only one specific design solution, but hiring a designer with a rich breadth of capabilities and experience that you can tap into repeatedly is a much wiser investment. As a solo small business owner, you have a vision, dream and direction for your business. The designer's job is to come alongside you and develop the best visual solution to fulfill that vision, dream and direction.

It is your image. It is your business's message that the designer will be communicating visually. Make sure whoever you hire aligns with the key points explained above. Hiring the right graphic designer or website designer really is that important.

Before you hire any graphic designer or web designer to help your solo small business, you *must* get a copy of my comprehensive special report: "How To Hire A Designer Without Getting Ripped Off." This report normally sells for $197, but as an owner of this book, it's one of my free gifts for you. The report will help ensure you hire the absolute best professional for the job. Visit: www.MarketingForSolos .com/book-gift to get your copy. ◆

Sometimes It's the Little Things

M arketing success is as much about perception and image as it is about choosing the right tools to use. Direct mail, referrals, a comprehensive, workhorse website, video and brochures are all great and necessary tools to help you market your solo small business. But, sometimes the little things make all the difference in the world when it comes to marketing and the success of your solo small business.

Projecting the Proper Perception

People's perceptions tend to become their reality. It's common to overlook the little things, but they can make all of the difference in the world to the success of your marketing and solo small business.

Carefully Choose the Words You Use

Don't say to prospects or clients things like, "My week is wide open," "I can fit you in whenever," "This is a slow time of year for me," or other similar things. This sends the wrong message to your prospects and clients. Why aren't you busy? Is it because you can't get any clients? If you really are as good at what you do as you say you are, wouldn't you be swamped with work?

Never communicate to a client or prospect that you have too much time on your hands. When booking appointments, offer two choices, not all day or all week. Watch what you say about the client load you currently have.

Value Your Work and Yourself

Don't charge too little for your services because you're new in business or you feel like you aren't worth more. This sends a message that makes prospects wonder why you charge so little. Is it because you don't value your work? Will I really get something cheap?

Charge what others in your industry charge. Don't set out to be the cheapest provider there is just to scoop up a lot of business. Nine times out of ten, cheap pricing will backfire on you.

Appear Successful, NEVER Needy

Don't look or act like you *need* business or clients. Always give the impression that you are booked, busy and sought after, even if you're not. This isn't to lie or be manipulative. It is to give the image that you are successful (plus, it also help you train your success mindset). Remember, people's perceptions tend to become their reality.

If you don't have clients and are panicked about it, share that with a spouse or close friend. Never ever let prospects or clients know this. No one wants to do business with a needy person. We all want to work with someone who is successful. You must communicate success to your clients and prospects.

Always Do What You Say You'll Do

Not doing what you say you will do is the fastest way to look like an unprofessional business owner with whom no one would want to work. It is absolutely essential that you indeed do what you tell people you will do. This is not just your image and professionalism on the line, but your integrity and reliability, as well. If you told a client that you would deliver a product on Monday at 3:30PM, then it had better be there no later than Monday at 3:30PM. If you tell a prospect that you will call her back in three weeks, it had better be no later than three weeks when she hears from you again. If you tell someone you are going to research a solution and provide a printout of various options, you must deliver. If you tell a potential client that you'll come to his or her house and deliver an estimate on a new deck, you'd better show up.

How many times has someone dropped the ball with you? How many times have you heard, "I'll do …" or "I'll be …" or "I'll get …" only to have it never happen? How do you feel when this happens? What do you think? Do you trust this person? Do you rely on this person? More than likely, no.

Now think about what your prospects or clients think of you if you don't do what you say you will do. You're just giving them a valid reason never to do business with you. Little things can make a big difference. It's *much* better to *not* tell a prospect or client that you'll do something, than to tell them, not do it and drop the ball. Telling people you'll do something, but never doing it will accomplish one thing—bankruptcy.

Be Professional When You Answer the Phone

During normal business hours, 8:00AM to 5:00PM, you should be in business mode, which means *not* answering the phone when you have distracting or unprofessional noises going on in the background. Just because the phone rings doesn't mean you have to answer it right then. It's much better to let the caller go to voice mail and call them back later, rather than answering with your four-year-old child screaming in the background. This should be obvious, but you'd be surprised how often it happens.

Way too many solo small business owners are guilty of this. Professional? Absolutely not. This is a biggie when it comes to the little things that can make a big difference.

I once called a prospective client around 2:00 in the afternoon. As we were talking, she suddenly exploded into a storm of profanities that would make a sailor blush. I listened on the phone, stunned, then cautiously asked, "What's wrong?" She said she was in the car, driving to an appointment and some guy just cut her off in traffic. Yikes! Needless to say, I chose *not* to work with her. Now, you may not commit an offense that bad when you answer the phone, but your dog barking or a vacuum cleaner running doesn't sound any more professional.

What does it say to your caller when they hear in the background, "Attention shoppers, today at Wal-Mart® toilet paper is on sale, two for $5.00?" It says you don't have enough business. Otherwise, why would you be at Wal-Mart during the workday? It's all about image. Do you sound professional? Or, do you sound like you work at "Romper Room" and have too much time on your hands? Save your image and the caller—pick up the caller's voice mail message and return the call later.

Make It Easy to Buy and to Pay

Do you offer your clients various payment methods, or do you "force" your clients to pay one way—and one way only? If you do the latter, you are more than likely turning away business without even knowing it. You must make it easy for people to buy from you, as well as pay you. What do I mean by this? Accept cash, check, money order and every major credit card—yes, even the ones who charge higher fees. Give your clients payment options and payment plans. Have gift certificates available. Rather than demanding one payment or two, offer to split payments into six, nine or even twelve payments. This is especially important if you charge a lot for your services.

Package your services into bundles and give an incentive for "buying in bulk." For example, a personal coach may charge $100 per coaching session, but if a client agrees to buy four sessions up front, he gets a $50 discount. This is a win-win for both—the coach gets money up front and the client gets a deal.

Be creative, offer options—many, many options. I work with small business owners whose budgets are usually very tight. I am by no means the cheapest person in town when it comes to graphic design, website design and marketing. Therefore, I offer my clients as many payment options as possible. The results? I have a lot of clients who may not have been able to work with me had I not offered options and payment plans. If you work with small businesses, especially solo small businesses, I *highly* recommend you do the same.

Keep Your Clients in the Loop

I'm sure you have taken your car to the shop for service or repair. If your car is really sick and needs work, what's usually the first thing you say to the mechanic, right after you explain what your car is doing? "Call me before you do anything." Right? You want to be in the loop. You want a heads-up before anything happens and money is spent without your authorization.

Your clients are exactly the same. They want to be informed, in the loop and given a heads-up. Sure, when you first work with a client, you more than likely explain the process by which you will work together, but do you follow up after that? Do you give status reports? Do you regularly let clients know where their project is, or tell or show them what you have done thus far?

I don't know about you, but when I spend money for a service, I expect to be kept up to date as to what is going on. I hate it when *I* am the one who has to call the business owner I am working with and ask, "Where are we with ___?" That's really unprofessional. Don't do that to your clients; keep them in the loop. I know you're busy. We're all busy. Your clients are busy, but if someone hires you and trusts you with their hard-earned money, don't keep them in the dark; keep them in the loop.

Avoid Negative Surprises

This relates to keeping your clients in the loop. Most people like surprises—positive surprises like the ones we discussed in Chapter 3. But many, if not all, people *hate* negative surprises. What's the difference? How about negative surprises such as: quoting your client a firm price, but when the job is done and it's time to collect … surprise! You end up charging the client $100 or more above the quote. You promise a job will be done for your client on a specific date … but, surprise! The date comes and goes, and you don't warn the client or explain the delay. Or, you go on vacation, but don't change your voice mail … and surprise! Your client doesn't know you're out of town and feels blown off when you don't return his phone calls.

Am I being harsh? No, not really. Every one of the three examples has happened to me and to colleagues and friends of mine. You may even have experienced something similar. These are negative surprises; they leave a negative feeling with your clients. Negative surprises always leave your client feeling, well, negative. When you're a solo small business, you always want to make your client feel important, valued and appreciated. Make sure that the only surprises you give your clients are ones that are positive and make them feel like the valuable assets they really are.

Thanking Clients

How do you thank clients for doing business with you? Is it just a simple "thanks," or do you make it a big deal and an extra point to show your clients just how much you appreciate them for their business? I mean, after all, they are paying your mortgage and putting food on your table, right? Make sure that you're not overlooking this "little thing." Thank clients for their business. Show them that you appreciate them.

One of the best ways to do this is with a handwritten note. I highly recommend that you use handwritten notes as much as possible to show your clients your appreciation. You can never send too many thank you notes. I send a handwritten thank you note each and every single time I get a new client and each and every time a client buys from me again. You can also thank clients in other ways, such as calling them up or, as I mentioned in Chapter 3, giving a small gift. However you choose to thank clients, thank them big. This is no time for little things.

A Final Example of the Little Things

I leave you with a great example of how taking care of the little things can have a huge impact on your bottom line. I found this in Dan S. Kennedy's book: *The Ultimate Marketing Plan: Find Your Most Competitive Edge, Turn it Into a Powerful Marketing Message and Deliver it to the Right Prospects.*

"Once I was counseling a chiropractor, brand new in his practice, located in a brand new shopping center at a busy intersection, but too new to be fully occupied with tenants. He was suffering an inordinately high number of 'no shows': people who would respond to his advertising, schedule exam appointments, then not show up. His parking lot was nude.

He and his staff parked their own cars behind the center. His practice was so new there were rarely patients' cars parked there. And there was no adjacent tenants creating traffic. 'How would you feel,' I asked him, 'if you started to drive up here for your first appointment?' We got his car, his staff's cars and a couple of rented-by-the-week Cadillacs parked in front of that office; his no-show rate dropped like a rock." [4]

Little things are powerful. If you are suffering with "no shows" of your own or can't seem to attract clients no matter how hard you try, take a fine-toothed comb and look at all of the little, seemingly insignificant details—the way you answer the phone, the way you shake hands, the way you thank someone, the way your office looks and more. All of these little items send messages to your prospects.

You need to constantly put yourself in the position of your prospects. Ask yourself, "Would I like this?" "Would I be comfortable with this?" "Does this make a good impression?" "Do I feel good with this?" Think and ask yourself, "If I were going to hire someone for this service (yours) would I hire me if I walked into this office and was treated the way I treat people?" If yes, fantastic, keep repeating the successful impression you have built. If no, change things, improve things immediately! Make sure the little things aren't sabotaging you.

Keep a close eye on the little things, they can make a world of difference as a solo small business owner! ◆

---

4 Dan S. Kennedy, *The Ultimate Marketing Plan: Find Your Most Promotable Competitive Edge, Turn It Into A Powerful Marketing Message, And Deliver It To The Right Prospects* (Avon, MA: Adams Media Corporation, 2000). Page 71.

Testing, Testing, Is This Thing On?

Don't even think of skipping this chapter. I know, I know: testing? Yuck! When most solo small business owners hear the word "test," they glaze over and think, "How the heck do I test? It's hard. It's a pain. It's boring, I hate it, It takes too much time …" and so on.

Testing is a huge part of successful marketing. And, I've got good news for you: it's easier than you think and is not as drudgery as you think either.

In this chapter, I will share with you some quick and easy ways to test your marketing activities, so you'll know what's working, what isn't, what to continue and what to drop.

You do want your hard work, effort and money spent on marketing to pay off, don't you? Then you must test.

Test, Test and Test Some More

I once heard Fred Gleeck*, a marketing consultant and informa-tion products guru say, "Measurement eliminates argument." That's a great saying, and it's really true. My question to you is, do you know what's working in your marketing? Do you know what message your prospects are attracted to? Do you know what tools your prospects are acting upon?

Really? Is this because you really know, because of testing; or do you do what most solo small business owners do, which is simply guess? I heard a saying once, "A wise man is he who knows he knows not." So the question is: how wise are you? Don't guess. Test, test and test some more.

Ask and You Shall Receive

The simplest way to test is to ask. Ask people you know—your existing clients, your past clients, your friends, your colleagues, your golf buddies, your book club, whoever you know. Ask, ask, ask, and you are testing, testing, testing. This is the easiest and cheapest mar-ket research you can do.

I do this all of the time in my small business, because, even though I may hate to admit it, I don't know all of the answers. Yes, it's true. I don't know everything. Sometimes I may think I do, but I would be wrong. If you think you know all the answers, my friend, you are wrong, too.

A mentor of mine, John Eggen* of Mission Publishing, taught me great wisdom about thinking you know all the answers and about ex-actly what will and will not work. John teaches:

*Fred Gleeck, www.FredGleeck.com.
*John Eggen, Mission Publishing, www.MissionPublishing.com.

"Marketing amateurs always think they know what will work and when they try something and it fails, they throw up their hands and give up forever. Marketing experts, on the other hand, always know that they don't know exactly what will work. Instead they start with time-tested tactics—things that are proven to work time and again in similar situations. Then, they eliminate the guesswork by approaching all their actions as tests and they simply let the marketplace vote with its voices and wallet on what works and what they want."

So, which do you want to be—a marketing amateur or a marketing expert? Unless you test, you're just an amateur.

This brings up some questions you may have about marketing in your industry. You may wonder, "What is the best vehicle to reach my target market? Advertising in the Yellow Pages? Direct mail? Talks? Workshops?" Want a great way to find out? Ask.

Ask your current and past clients:
➤ How did you find me?
➤ If you did not know that I existed, and were looking for me, where would you look?
➤ What attracted you to my services?

Ask friends, family, associates and colleagues:
➤ Where would you look to find my type of business?
➤ What types of offers would you respond to?
➤ What marketing activities would grab your attention?

Don't just think you know the answers. Test. Ask. Ask some more. Ask as many questions as you can think of and as many questions as you can get answers to.

Let me give you an example. Recently, I was giving a talk on "Big Marketing Mistakes Solo Small Business Owners Make." After my talk, I spent about 30 minutes helping the audience with marketing problems, issues and questions. A young woman raised her hand and said, "I am starting a nail salon, and I want to know what I should put in my Yellow Page ad."

I asked her, "Are you sure that a Yellow Page ad is the best vehicle for marketing yourself?" "Well, yeah," she responded. "How do you know?" I asked. She said, "Well, I have always heard that all store fronts or retail types of businesses should advertise in the Yellow Pages." I said, "You're making a common marketing mistake and that is, you're guessing. You're guessing that a Yellow Page ad is the best marketing avenue for your clientele. You're guessing that, since it works for other types of retail businesses, it will work for you. You need to test. In fact, why don't we do a little test right now."

I then asked the audience of about 25–30 people, "Ladies in the audience—and gentlemen who like to have their nails done—if you were looking for a nail salon, would you look in the Yellow Pages to find a salon?" NO WAY was the overwhelming answer from the audience. "Wow," the young woman said. "I had no idea."

This is a very common mistake; it is also very easy to fix: just test. You and I don't know all of the answers. We don't know every single time what will and will not work. Test.

Tools to Help You Test

There are numerous, inexpensive ways to test. Here are three tools that can help you:

Tool #1: Website Statistics

There are tons of free and inexpensive website statistic tools. These allow you to see how much traffic you are generating, where clients are coming from, what pages they are viewing, how long they stay at your site and what page they leave from. Armed with this information, you can study which pages on your site are successful and which need tweaking. For instance, if you see that 45% of your website visitors are coming to your site via your home page (called the entry page) and 40% of those visitors are leaving your home page (called the exit page) without clicking on any other pages, you know that you need to tweak the home page so it'll better convince visitors to explore your website further.

Tool #2: Surveys

It's easy and inexpensive to conduct a survey of your current and past clients, as well as prospects or colleagues who can give you good information for your marketing. Simply type up a few questions on your letterhead and mail them out to those whose feedback you want.

A few things to keep in mind about surveys ...

➤ If you mail the survey, include a self-addressed stamped envelope, so recipients don't have to furnish their own stamp or look up your address. This will increase your response rate.

➤ It is best to have the survey remain anonymous, so that participants feel that they can be honest and forthcoming with their answers.

➤ If you don't want to type up a survey, hire someone to call your audience and ask them the survey questions. But, be careful: make sure that you don't take up too much of their time and that your caller isn't pushy or demanding. They are volunteering their time to answer your questions. They don't *have* to do this for you.

➤ If you can offer a free gift for taking the survey, all the better. A small thank-you gift of some kind. Movie tickets, gift cards, articles or special reports will show your appreciation for their time and increase your response as well.

➤ There are various online services that you can use to develop and distribute surveys via email and the web. Again, be very careful. Get permission before you email your audience, or you could be accused of spamming, which would actually cause more harm than good. I highly recommend that you use methods other than email for surveys, but it can be a good avenue if you have explicit permission from your audience.

Tool #3: Feedback Forms

When you finish working with a client, do you ask them for feedback on the job you did? If not, you are missing great nuggets of information that can improve your marketing and the services you provide. Make it a habit to ask every client to give you their feedback once the job is done. Ask them to be open and honest, as you want to continually provide the best service possible and need their feedback to do so.

Asking questions such as how you did with the job is obvious, but don't forget to get feedback on things such as price, payment options, the speed of service, the time it took from start to finish, other offerings they would like to see, other ways to package services, and anything else that would help you to better meet their needs.

How Do You Know Which Marketing Activities to Continue?

A good marketing activity is one that you can repeat and continue. The best and simplest way to decide which activities you should repeat is to look to past success.

Look Back to Move Forward

Take a look at your client roster. Where do most of your clients come from? Referrals, networking, your comprehensive, workhorse website, direct mail campaigns, what? Whatever source generated the most clients for you is obviously one to repeat, but you can take it one step further and explore the specific details of that source.

For example, instead of just noting that most of your clients come from networking events, note the specific details about which networking events generate the most clients. Repeat this process with one to four other successful client sources, again noting the specific details of each source. So, if networking was #1, what are the specific details of networking that generated you clients? If your website was #2, what are the specific details of your website that generated clients? Was it your eZine? Articles you wrote? Or did you get most clients after the free tele-seminar you hosted? And so on, through your history.

When you finish this exercise, you will have the specific details of the top two to five sources that generate you the most clients. Having these two to five successes in front of you will keep you focused on repeating your success, and help eliminate sporadic, chaotic marketing. You will know the specifics of what has worked in the past, and you'll generate consistent results by consistently repeating these activities over and over and over again.

One of my clients is a chiropractic center. They are very involved with BNI, the referral group I told you about earlier, and they've generated a lot of business from referrals as a result of their involvement.

One thing BNI encourages is that its members meet with other members outside of the group for what's called a "one-on-one meeting." This helps members get to know each other's businesses better, in order to generate better referrals, in a setting other than the ninety-minute weekly meeting. The chiropractic center had been doing one-on-one meetings consistently for a while, but as things got busier and busier, the one-on-one meetings got fewer and fewer.

Upon looking at their history and which sources most of their clients came from, they noticed that, when they did a lot of one-on-one meetings, they got a lot more referrals. When they did fewer one-on-one meetings, they got fewer referrals. Had they simply listed the #1 source of business as BNI, but not dug a little deeper to see that not just BNI, but BNI with lots of one-on-one meetings was the #1 source of their business, they would not have fully understood the measure of success. With this deeper knowledge, they made a commitment that, no matter how busy they get, they will continue the one-on-one meetings on a weekly basis.

You need to do the same digging. Don't stop at: "My #1 source of business is networking." Dig deeper: what type of networking, what day of the week, what time of year, etc. The more you know, the more you can replicate past success, and the more successful you will be.

Some say knowledge is power. I say *very detailed* knowledge is marketing power.

What if You're a Brand New Business?

Looking to past success is great, but what if you're a brand new solo small business owner and have no past results or history to glean from? There are four steps to handling testing and replicating success for the newbies:

Step 1: Ask and Think

If you're new in business, you need to ask questions, and you need to ask the right questions. As we discussed before, ask everyone you know questions such as: Where would you look to find a business like mine? What would you look for? What would you respond to?

Along with asking comes thinking. Think about your potential clients. What are they looking for? Where are they located? How can you reach them? Think about yourself. If you were looking for a service like the one you provide, where would you look? If you would never look in the Yellow Pages, then don't focus efforts on that type of advertising. If you would respond to a direct mail postcard, think of how you can develop a campaign to reach your target market. Asking questions and thinking about where your prospects will find you are the first steps in testing what will work for you.

Step 2: Try and See

After you have asked and thought, the next step is to try and see if it works. Develop your marketing materials and activities, get them out there to your prospects, then try them out and see what happens.

Step 3: Test and Tweak

Once you have begun your marketing activities, the next step is to test and tweak. If you try a direct mail campaign, test various offers. What is working? What are people responding to? Tweak your materials to follow your testing results. If you are actively networking or are active in a referral group, which commercials work best for you? What gets the prospect to ask the all-important question of "How do you do that?" Tweak your efforts, materials and presentation until you have clear winners.

Step 4: Track and Repeat

After about six months to one year in business, you will have some history that you can pull from. You will be able to look at your current and past clients and begin digging to see what has worked and the details behind the successes. Then you will be able to list the top two to five sources for most of your business and continue with these activities for long-term results.

Proof that Testing Works

Corporate America spends billions of dollars a year on testing, everything from focus groups to split-run advertising.

The following is a fun and great example from corporate America that illustrates the value and the power of testing.

Kleenex® was originally invented to remove cold cream and was originally advertised as a makeup removal tissue. After the Kleenex manufacturer, Kimberly-Clark Corporation, learned that people were using the product to blow their noses, they decided to do an advertising test in Peoria, Illinois newspapers. They ran two similar ads stressing the two uses of Kleenex and asked readers to respond.

The result: 60% used Kleenex to blow their noses. The advertising was changed and sales doubled, proving that testing works. Kleenex thought it had a winner with a makeup and cold cream removal tissue; the marketplace proved them wrong. [5]

Those are pretty incredible results. In retrospect, it seems obvious, but without testing, millions of dollars would have been lost. If testing is good enough for corporate America, isn't it good enough for your solo small business? Test, track, tweak, and you *will* profit! ◆

---

5 Source: About.com (www.About.com), Inventors Section, History of Kleenex.

Lather, Rinse, Repeat

S uccessful marketing is about the long haul, the long-term relationship, the long-term commitment. It's not about a one-
time shot. The key is repetition. Repetition is a fundamental ingredi-
ent in successful marketing. Repetition is the lather, rinse and repeat
of your solo small business. You must market over and over and over
again.

Once Is NEVER Enough

There is a mistake that too many solo small business owners
make: developing a marketing piece, mailing it out once to their target audience, getting little or no response and then quitting.

Sending out something once hardly, if ever, works. I once heard of
a *very* large business that sent out something one time and got a hoard

of sales; but I have only heard of this once and the offer was so dang incredible that a vast majority of small businesses could never afford to do it. The offer was for a free Rolex® watch if the prospects bought by a certain date. This large business sent out their promotion once and it worked, but this happens very, very rarely, and no small business should be fooled into thinking it can do the same … unless, of course, you have the money to promote an unbelievable offer like this.

It Isn't Sexy, But It Is Successful

Let me let you in on a little secret of marketing when you're a solo small business owner. Successful marketing is not all that sexy or glamorous. Sorry, it just isn't. Successfully marketing your services is not about one-time things. It's a long, nurturing, continuous relationship. It's developing marketing strategies to use again and again and again.

Think about most marketers you run into. It's often a one-time thing—they send you one mailing that asks for your business and your money and then bam, they're gone. That is *not* how successful marketing works. It's not about a one-night stand. It is about building trust, understanding and relationships. And that takes time.

Marketing Is a Process

Marketing is a process, not an event. Marketing is ongoing and constant. Marketing is like marriage; you have to keep at it to make it grow, thrive and prosper.

How would your relationship with a loved one be if you only spoke to them once (think sending out a one-time mailing and never mailing again)? Or how would that relationship be if you only communicated with your loved one when you needed money (think only talking to your past clients when you need more business)? Marketing is a relationship, and just like a real-life relationship, it must be nurtured and worked on. The reason why so many small businesses fail at marketing is because they fail to realize the fundamental fact that marketing is like a relationship. If you don't consistently work on it, feed it, clothe it, hold it, spend time with it and hold it dear, it will fail.

The Long Haul and Long-Term Commitment

I run into a lot of solo small business owners who tell me marketing doesn't work. Upon further investigation, I learn why *their* marketing doesn't work: they fail at the marketing fundamental of repetition and being in it for the long haul.

What usually happens is they design a postcard, flyer, sales letter, coupon, etc., then mail it out to a list of people just once and either A: expect the phone to ring off the hook or B: they "just want to see if it will work."

More times than not, it doesn't work, simply because there are so many things fighting for a prospect's time that a one-time thing stands little chance. So the solo small business owner throws up his hands and shouts, "Marketing is hard. Marketing doesn't work. Why should I spend any more energy on marketing if it doesn't work?"

When I hear these stories, I can't help but think, "Duh." Of course, the one-time approach doesn't work. Think about this: do you really believe that a mother of four, who is a successful corporate executive, who stumbles in the door with an armful of mail after a hard day at the office will remember your one postcard she saw one time when she was completely exhausted from the day? Of course not. You're kidding yourself if you think once will work.

Once, twice, three times—it's still not enough. Repetition is just that—repetition. You must market again and again and again and again and again and again and again and again. And again.

Repetition Is a Relationship

What kind of a relationship would you have with your best friends if you only talked to them one time a year? You probably wouldn't be best friends for too long, would you? When marketing your solo small business, approach it as building a relationship.

Most solo small business owners talk to their potential best friends (prospective clients) only one time. Big mistake. The key to repetition is hanging in there for the long haul ... the very long haul. You will get frustrated. You will want to give up. But don't. Keep going. Building a relationship takes time. Prospects need to see your message over and over and over and over again before they even begin to get the message. You must keep up the repetition and momentum.

Too many small business owners originally commit to the long-haul, but midway through, they give up. If you only send something out once, don't commit to the long-haul and fail to build a relationship, how will you test your marketing activities? How will you know what works? How will you know what to tweak? How will you know what to keep doing to replicate success?

Marketing is a lot like dating, you have to work at it. If you walked up to someone you didn't know and asked them, "Will you marry me?" They'd probably slap you. Yet every day solo small business owners market themselves in this way. They approach their prospective clients *one* time and ask for marriage. This approach never works very well.

How Many, How Much and How Long?

So, how much repetition is needed? How long do you have to commit to building a relationship before a prospect becomes a client? How many times does a prospect have to see your message before they 'get it' and pick up the phone? There are many conflicting answers out there. But, as I mentioned before, marketing research and most industry experts have concluded that, on average, people must see a marketing message *nine times* before they even understand what is going on enough to consider making a purchase. That's nine with an 'n.'

I think this is the best illustration of how essential it is for you to market to your prospects again and again and again:

1. The first time a man looks at an advertisement, he does not see it.
2. The second time, he does not notice it.
3. The third time, he is conscious of its existence.
4. The fourth time, he faintly remembers having seen it before.
5. The fifth time, he reads it.
6. The sixth time, he turns up his nose at it.
7. The seventh time, he reads it through and says, "Oh brother!"
8. The eighth time, he says, "Here's that confounded thing again!"
9. The ninth time, he wonders if it amounts to anything.
10. The tenth time, he asks his neighbor if he has tried it.
11. The eleventh time, he wonders how the advertiser makes it pay off.
12. The twelfth time, he thinks it must be a good thing.
13. The thirteenth time, he thinks perhaps it might be worth something.

14. The fourteenth time, he remembers wanting such a thing for a long time.
15. The fifteenth time, he is tantalized because he cannot afford to buy it.
16. The sixteenth time, he thinks he will buy it some day.
17. The seventeenth time, he makes a memorandum to buy it.
18. The eighteenth time, he swears at his poverty.
19. The nineteenth time, he counts his money carefully.
20. The twentieth time he sees the ad, he buys what it is offering.

This was written by Thomas Smith of London, England in 1885! And it is as true today is it was over 100 years ago. Repetition works. Lather, rinse, repeat!

Think about it: you and I aren't any different. We need to see things over and over and over again before they really register. I guarantee you, this applies to your prospects, as well. You must market to them again and again and again.

People forget. In fact, they forget so often and so easily that it's a little scary. Don't believe me? Let me challenge you. I want you to answer the following: name one commercial you saw on television three days ago during prime time. Name just one. What was the commercial? What was it selling? What was the company or product being advertised? If you don't watch TV, tell me about an ad you heard on the radio. Or tell me everything you ate three days ago. I mean everything. Breakfast, lunch, dinner, snacks and drinks.

Can you do it? No? Okay, how about two days ago? One day ago? One hour ago? See what I mean? I ask a lot of groups and small business owners this question, and 95% of the time, not one person can name even one single commercial from three days ago, or even two days ago or even one day ago. And yet, solo small business owners think their prospects will remember.

How Frequently?

I tell all of my clients to plan their marketing activities for a bare minimum of six months. This would be one time per month for six months to the *same* group of people. So you would design and plan a direct mail campaign, you'd buy the list and then mail the campaign to them once a month for six months. Again this is bare minimum.

The best strategy, if your budget allows for it, is to plan and market to a single group for at least one year. Once a month, for twelve months, to the same people. That will be twelve times that a prospect will see your message.

This may seem like a lot, but keep in mind all that we've discussed so far. Again and again and again is key. Something else you need to remember is: if you're buying a mailing list of prospects to send your campaign to, it will be a cold list, meaning the prospects do not know anything about you. Thus, you will need to mail to these prospects numerous times to build a relationship with them.

If you will be mailing to your house list (your own list of current and past clients), you can probably drop the number of times you mail to them, since they already know who you are. However, don't let the fact that you are using your house list be an excuse to mail only once, twice or just a few times. Even those who know you (and hopefully love you) still need to see your message over and over again.

When I coach solo small business owners about how often to mail, the biggest complaint (and excuse) I hear is, "I don't have the money to market once a month for a year, or even for six months." My answer is simply that you have to. Period. Some way, somehow, you must lather, rinse and repeat over and over again.

Focus, Focus, Focus (Again)

Your budget is set, your plan is ready and you're going to market for at least six months. So who do you market to? Rather than buy a list of 2,000 names in a five-mile radius of your location and send out twelve impersonal mailings, focus your efforts.

Remember that niche that you've now developed? Focus on your niche, and your results will be much, much better. Just because you will be marketing over and over and over again, don't forget about the fundamentals of targeting a specific niche and dominating it.

If budget is a huge concern, here is something to implant into your brain forever … it will *always* be better and more effective if you market to *fewer* people *more* often, than it is to market to *more* people *less* often.

So if you can afford to mail one postcard to 10,000 prospects, don't! Instead mail ten postcards to 1,000 prospects and your results will significantly increase!

Do your research. Do your homework. Make sure the people you are targeting are qualified to be good clients. Make sure they are in the niche you want to target. Make your message personal. Make it of value. Address the prospects' 3Ps. Use everything you have learned thus far. That way you'll ensure an effective use of your limited funds.

This focused technique really works.

A personal trainer had a very limited budget, but really focused his efforts on a specific niche, and in doing so, achieved excellent results. This trainer was fairly new in business, and like so many other small businesses, he had very little extra cash to play with. But, he decided to focus his efforts.

First he picked a niche to pursue. He loves to play golf and is a really, really good golfer. He had found that certain exercises and types of weight-lifting improved his own game substantially. He had also worked with several friends who were golfers, with great results. So he decided to target golfers. His approach was to help golfers whose swing and game were suffering.

He worked out a budget to target this market niche for at least one year (one time per month for twelve months). He went to see his golf instructor at the course where he regularly played and worked out a deal to purchase the names of 75 members who fit the profile of his perfect client.

He then developed twelve very valuable articles, reports and case studies for his market. These articles, reports and case studies were loaded with valuable information on how to shave strokes off your golf game, how to improve the mechanics of a swing, etc. But the key was that the information all related to his personal training techniques—showing the prospects exactly how they would benefit and their golf game would improve through the exercises and weight-lifting regimen he had developed.

He mailed out these materials once a month for twelve months. As is typically the case, it took a little time before he got a response. The prospects had to see his material over and over and over again. But, he kept at it, and for a small investment of marketing dollars, he got a handful of really good, long-term clients. He told me that he started seeing most of the results toward the end of his mailings. For him, things started happening after about the seventh or eighth mailing. He even had one client tell him that he had received his information and read through some of it, but didn't really believe that lifting weights could make a difference. But, the more he read, the more he thought, "What do I have to lose? I might as well give this guy a try." And he did. He actually ended up being one of the personal trainer's best clients and referred a few of his golf buddies, to the trainer as well.

So, what if the personal trainer had gotten frustrated and quit after mailing number three, six, seven or even eleven? He probably would have missed out.

Stay in there, lather, rinse, repeat again and again. Repetition. It really works!

There's an old Chinese proverb that says, "The temptation to quit will be greatest just before you're about to succeed." I have this quote taped to my computer screen, and I read it every single day. It's true. If you quit, you may well have quit just a split second before the floodgates were going to open. Repetition and a long-term commitment guard against that.

Let me give you one final example: me. When I purchased my first home it needed new windows. I remember I used to hear commercials on the radio for this guy who would say, "If you've gotten a quote for new windows and were blown away by the price, give me a call. I guarantee I will save you at least 30%." I heard these ads all the time, but I wasn't ready to purchase yet. Well, now I no longer hear these ads. Were they so successful that the guy doesn't advertise any more—which is a mistake, as illustrated here? Or did he give up and stop, abandoning the long haul? I have no idea. In the time that has passed, I have forgotten the guy's name and company. If he were still advertising, I would have given him a call. Had he continued to advertise, when the time was right for me, he could have had another client.

How do you know when the time will be right for your prospects? Will it be the third time they see your message? The fifth? The tenth? You cannot afford *not* to lather, rinse and repeat! ◆

 Key Concept

Lather, Rinse, Repeat: Marketing is a long-term relationship that you have to stay with and not give up on. Sending out your marketing messages once or twice hardly ever works. I know it can be sometimes frustrating to stick it out, but the whole "get rich quick thing" umm, yeah that's a lie. Consistent marketing and repetition over the long-term works!

Consistency Is Key

Consistency is another very important factor in the long-term success of your marketing activities and efforts. It is a fundamental principle that, unfortunately, many solo small businesses do not understand. Consistency goes hand in hand with the previous fundamental principle we talked about—repetition.

Why Should You Care About Consistency?

Why is consistency such a big deal? Why should you care? Well, for starters, no one likes inconsistent results or inconsistent rules or inconsistent people or inconsistent anything, for that matter.

Inconsistency in your image and activities will be perceived as a big negative to your prospects. Another way to think about consistency is tradition. Think about a great tradition you have with your family or friends. How does it make you feel? Comfortable? Secure? Loved? Appreciated? Valued? Isn't that tradition something you look forward to? And if, for some reason, the tradition doesn't happen at the time it always does, don't you feel a little discombobulated? I know I do.

It's the same with your prospects. Inconsistency jars people, even if it is subtle. People want and need consistency in their lives. It is a huge value. This is why consistency is *so* important.

There are three main areas where your small business must be consistent ...

1. Consistency in your image.
2. Consistency in your activities.
3. Consistency in when you market.

Consistency in Your Image

Take a moment and pull out all of the marketing materials you currently have. Go ahead ... I'll wait. Pull out everything—your brochure, your business card, your letterhead, your envelope, your fax cover sheet. If you have a website, log on so it is visible on your computer monitor. If you have a price sheet, contract, or other sales materials, get them out, too. Pull out any and *all* of the materials you use in your small business. I mean everything, be it small or large, everything you use in the day-to-day operations and marketing of your small business. Spread all of these materials out on a table. Now—what do you see?

➤ Do you see two or three different fonts?

➤ Do you see four or five different colors?

➤ Do you see different versions of your logo?

➤ Do you see different versions of your brochure?

➤ Is the pile of materials a complete hodgepodge of chaos?

If you answered yes to any of the above questions, you have an image consistency problem—and that's a very big problem.

When you look at the mass of materials in front of you, you should see one thing: consistency—a consistent, cohesive image.

You should see the same font used on everything, *not* one font on your brochure and a completely different font on your flyers and yet another completely different font on your pocket folder—the same font on *everything*. You should see the same colors used on everything—not blue on your website and green on your sales flyer and purple in your brochure and yellow on your price sheet—the same colors on *everything*.

When you look at the pile of materials in front of you, everything—and I mean everything—should look like it came from the same business. Consistency. Consistency. Consistency. I think you get my point.

Consistency with your image is key. It is *not* okay to change fonts and change colors and change versions of your materials whenever you feel like it. A consistent image builds confidence in prospects and in your existing clients. They know you. They know what you look like. They know your image.

Think about Coca-Cola® for a minute. What is their consistent image? Red, the script logo and the wave. Oh, and don't forget their uniquely shaped bottle. Everything Coca-Cola does with their image is consistent. What would you think if you saw the Coca-Cola logo in purple or yellow, or the shape of their bottle changed every time you saw it in the grocery store? You would definitely be a little puzzled and wonder what their problem was. In fact, you probably wouldn't buy the product because you'd be confused; sales would drop, and Coca-Cola would be in trouble. The same is true for your business.

You want to get to the point where every single client and prospect who sees your image recognizes it. An inconsistent image makes you look like an inconsistent person. Is that how you want people to see you? A consistent image will burn the image of your small business into the minds of your prospects. You will be memorable and easily recognized. How in the world do you expect people to remember you if every time they see a marketing piece from your solo small business, it looks completely different?

Consistency in one's image is a mark of a true professional. It says to your prospects and clients, "I care about how I look and how my business is perceived." If your image is inconsistent, you're telling your prospects and existing clients that you really don't care. You don't care about building their confidence. You aren't as "together" as you say you are. You aren't the expert that they should be working with. Worst of all, an inconsistent image makes you look like a complete fly-by-night amateur. Boy, that will really bring in the business, won't it?

A consistent image really is utterly, massively, totally, and incredibly important. Don't take lightly how damaging an inconsistent image can be to the success of your solo small businesses. "Oh, come on, Jeanna, consistency really isn't that important." Think about this for a moment: why would members of corporate America spend millions and billions of dollars to ensure that they have a consistent image in every aspect of their business, in every country in which they operate? Because consistency really is that important. Is your image consistent? If your marketing materials are a hodgepodge of mixed looks, it's time to change things.

Just Starting Out? Start Out with Consistency

If you are just starting out, get your image off on the right foot by making sure every single thing related to your business's image is consistent. Here are a few tips:

Hire a Professional Graphic Designer

Hire a professional graphic designer to design your marketing materials. See Chapter 9 for help on finding the right graphic designer or website designer for your solo small business.

Don't Tinker

After a professional designs your marketing materials, stop tweaking, playing with or revising the look of your materials. The worst thing you can do is pay a professional to design your logo and then keep tinkering with it. It dilutes your image and wastes the money you just spent on a professional design. You'd be surprised how often I see this happen. Sure, you can tweak the text of your website or brochure; but for the look of your materials, have them designed, then stop tinkering with them.

Pick a Font and Stick with It

Use that font for every single thing you send out from your business. Use it on your fax cover sheet, on your memos, on your flyers, on your letters, on your contracts, on everything. Every single company in corporate America has a corporate font, and that is all they use. You need a corporate font for your small business. Whatever font you choose when you get your materials professionally designed, stick with it. If Helvetica is what you choose, don't you dare mail, fax or send something out set in Times Roman.

Pick a Color or Set of Colors and Stick with It

Every company in corporate America has a corporate color; you need the same for your solo small business. If the color of your logo is cherry red, then always use cherry red. Not red-orange, not a pinkish red. Cherry red. You should pick and always use PMS colors and their RGB and CMYK equivalents for your business. PMS stands for Pantone® Matching System. PMS colors are the printing industry standard for color specification. For example, one of the PMS colors I use for my small business is PMS 200, which is a nice, deep red. I can print my business cards in Phoenix and my stationery in Chicago, and the colors will match, as long as I specify PMS 200 with both printers.

When you work with a professional graphic designer for your marketing materials, he or she will help you pick a PMS color or colors for your business. I also mentioned the RGB and CMYK equivalents for the PMS colors you choose. RGB stands for Red, Green and Blue, which are the three colors that are used to reproduce color on a computer screen, such as what you see on the Internet, or on a television. CMYK stands for Cyan, Magenta, Yellow and Black which are the four colors that are used to reproduce colors and images on printed materials, such as a brochure or flyer. You need to know these color equivalents. If your logo is going to appear on a computer screen (as on your website), you'll know how much Red, Green and Blue to specify so that the color of your logo will be consistent. It's the same with the CMYK equivalents for certain print work. Using my red as an example again, PMS 200 would have an RGB equivalent of R=219 G=0 B=41. So when I use my logo on my website, that is the color combination I specify in my web design program to use on the Internet. The CMYK equivalent is $C=0$ $M=100$ $Y=63$ $K=12$. I specify this combination of colors in the graphic design program I use for printed materials.

Use a Guideline Sheet

One last thing I recommend to ensure a consistent image: type up, or better yet, have your graphic designer type up a short guideline sheet that lists the fonts you use, the colors you use and the proper way to display your business' logo. Give a copy of this sheet to anyone who creates *any* marketing materials for your business. Even if they will only be creating a quick flyer, they'll need the guideline sheet to know what the rules of your small business image are. Don't let anyone send out anything that represents your company that violates the guidelines you've established. Some companies in corporate America fine employees or vendors who violate their guidelines.

Consistency in Your Marketing Activities

In marketing your solo small business, consistently doing more of the same is much better than doing a little bit of everything. Too often, I see solo small businesses doing a little bit of everything to market their businesses. Their marketing efforts go something like this: Create a flyer. Send out the flyer. Didn't get much response, so create a postcard. Send out the postcard. Didn't get much response, so find a networking event to attend. Attend networking event. Didn't get much response, so create an ad. Run the ad. Didn't get much response, so create a brochure. Mail out the brochure. Didn't get much response, so …. Get the picture? I call this Marketing A.D.D.

(Marketing Attention Deficit Disorder). Unfortunately it plagues a lot of solo small businesses. There's not a pill to take, but if you're looking for the cure … it's consistency. Of course you don't suffer from Marketing A.D.D., right?

Most marketing that solo small businesses do is all over the map. This little-bit-of-everything, A.D.D. approach generates very limited results. The key is consistently doing more of the same. You need to find three to six marketing activities that work and consistently do those activities over and over and over and over again. Remember that repetition thing we talked about in Chapter 12? How about strategically diversifying in Chapter 7?

More of the same—consistently—is far better than a little bit of everything. The obvious caveat is to do more of the same with the successful marketing activities you learned about in Chapter 8.

Consistency in When You Market

The final aspect of consistency is to be consistent in your marketing, meaning, marketing when you're busy and when you're not. One of the big reasons that solo small businesses get caught in what I call the feast-and-famine roller-coaster of inconsistent results and income is: when they get busy with clients, their marketing activities stop. Big mistake.

Make a point to schedule marketing on a weekly or—when you're just starting out—a daily basis. In fact, do it right now. Take out your calendar and schedule one hour this week to do absolutely nothing but work on your marketing. Then flip over to the next week and schedule the same. Schedule the rest of your year this way, and I promise you will get results.

Keep this appointment, no matter what. Make it a habit, and don't miss it for anything. Don't allow any distractions to derail you—

no phone calls, email or writing letters, unless it's marketing-related. Don't clean your desk, don't organize your bookshelf. Focus only on your marketing.

From this consistent, weekly appointment, you'll get in the habit of marketing in good times and in bad, in slow times and in fast. And as a result, you won't have to ride that feast-and-famine roller-coaster anymore.

If you struggle with this whole consistency thing, check out the Marketing for Solos® Academy. Membership in this dynamic program gives you personal guidance, mentoring, teaching, resources and accountability to help keep you plugged in and motivated, so you can market your services successfully *and* consistently. Visit the website: www.MarketingForSolosAcademy.com for details and information. ◆

Key Concept

Consistency is Key: Consistency in your image, in your marketing activities and when you market yourself is the key to long-term results and success. If you've been suffering from Marketing A.D.D. or you "forget" and get "too busy" to market yourself consistently, it's now time to stop, refocus and recommit. Doing so will make a big difference in the success of your solo small business!

Remember Where You Came From

Perhaps you have heard that it's a lot cheaper to keep a client and have them buy from you again and again than it is for you to go out and get a brand new client. It's true.

Once you've got clients, you have got to work to keep them. If you don't, you're really missing out and giving your existing and past clients a very easy and simple reason to do business with someone else.

Do you realize and understand that your existing and past clients are the reason that you are in business? Think about it. Essentially, these clients of yours have paid for your house, your car, your food, your clothing, your "grown up toys," your vacations and more. What possessions and success you have are more than likely a direct result of your clients.

Too many solo small business owners forget this. Too many solo small business owners take their existing and past clients for granted. This is a big, big mistake.

Market to Existing and Past Clients

It takes a lot less time, money, energy and resources to keep a client than it does to get a new one. Past clients already know you and—if you've provided them great service—trust you. You don't have to sell them again.

Securing a new client is harder, more expensive and time consuming. You have to spend money on marketing, you have to spend time talking with and building a relationship with a prospect before they become a client.

With all of this in mind, it never ceases to amaze me how many small business owners don't remember where they've come from, meaning they forget to continually market to their existing and past clients.

It doesn't matter if your business is set up so that clients can only make a one-time purchase of your services, you should always market to your past clients. You're wasting a huge opportunity by failing to do so. Past clients can be sold more of your services, higher priced services, and be a wellspring of referrals for you.

Your past clients have the potential to buy from you over and over and over again. You're leaving money—a lot of money—on the table if you don't continually market to them.

How Often Should Past Clients Hear from Me?

How often should you market to past clients? I have had some small business owners say to me, "I do market to my past clients. I send them a Christmas card each year." That's great, but sending a card once a year is the absolute minimum you should do.

Your past clients need to hear from you more than once a year, or they will forget about you, just as a prospect would if you sent them a marketing piece only once.

You should market to your past clients as often as possible, once every quarter is bare minimum; but just like marketing to prospects, marketing to your past clients once every month is much better. That way you are never out of their mind. They will never forget about you.

Remember: people forget. Even your past clients will forget you. What happens if they have a need, but haven't heard from you in months or years? Will they call you up again, or will they call the other business that has been hard at work marketing to them over the past months? Good question. It's hard to say, but that's a gamble I wouldn't want to take.

What To Do for Marketing

There are thousands of ways you can market to existing and past clients. The key is to find avenues and activities that fit with your personality and your budget, and are things that you can keep up with and continue, consistently. Do a little creative brainstorming and think to yourself, "Would I want to receive this type of marketing?" If yes, you may have a winner. If no, it's time to go back to the drawing board.

Bare Minimum ... Thanking Clients

The minute you get a new client, you need to send them a handwritten thank you note. Yes, you read that right—a handwritten thank you note. It doesn't have to be a novel, but a short little "John, I just wanted to thank you for your business. I look forward to working with you over the next four weeks ..." handwritten note will go a long way to build trust and camaraderie.

The minute you are finished working with a client, they should get another handwritten note. Again, it can be something short and sweet, such as, "John, it was a pleasure working with you. Thanks again, and I look forward to helping you again soon." This seals the deal. It says, not only do I appreciate your business, but I really appreciated working with you.

If you do nothing else but send these two handwritten thank you notes to your clients, I guarantee you will stand out from 99% of all the other small businesses out there. Try it; you'll be amazed at the response. Don't be surprised if you get a phone call or two from your clients thanking you for thanking them!

I know of a newer solo small business owner who really "gets it" when it comes to marketing to existing clients using this "thank you" approach. She is a massage therapist. For *every single* client, she picks up the phone and calls the day after their massage. This is huge! How many other small business owners do you know and use who actually call you on the phone to thank you for your business and check in to make sure everything went well?! I guarantee that this seemingly small act will be remembered and appreciated.

After you're done with the project or service you have provided, you can stay in contact with past clients in a number of ways: a newsletter (either printed and mailed or an electronic eZine), periodic cards, small gifts such as a gift card for coffee or movie tickets, periodic sales "coupons" exclusively for past clients, and even a client appreciation get-together.

I know a Realtor who is an avid golfer (I have no idea how he could be any good at golf, since he is very successful and busy with real estate all of the time). Every year, he has a client golf get-together where he invites all of his past clients to a very nice golf course for lunch and a round of nine holes as a thank you for their business. It's a huge success, and his past clients look forward to it every year. He has even told me that new clients get word of this event and ask him early on in their working relationship, "I get to come to the golf thing, right?"

Thanking your existing and past clients is the bare minimum marketing you should be doing when your small business is you.

Gifts and Goodies

Giving existing and past clients something for the Christmas holiday is obvious—and I mean more than just a card. Anyone can send a card. Stand out. Get creative. Can you send something else? I usually send very nice food and wine gift baskets or, at the very least, a gift card of some sort. My clients have commented on how much they love these items.

I know others who host luncheons or send wine, Christmas tree ornaments, home-baked cookies, office-related gifts such as nice pens, briefcases, etc. I even knew one solo small business owner who gave Apple® iPods to all of her clients when iPods were first released and first became popular. They were a huge hit.

When thinking of what types of gifts or goodies to give your clients, keep a few things in mind.

How many past clients do you have?

This will determine how much you can and probably should spend. If you have several hundred or even several thousand clients—which many independent insurance agents and other types of small businesses have—you may only be able to stuff your card with a gift card or some other small gift.

Do you have a smaller number of past clients who have spent a lot of money with you?

If so, you may want to look at something on the higher end. Obviously, your gift shouldn't bankrupt you, but it should be nice and thoughtful enough to get noticed and be memorable, and, above all, make your past client feel appreciated.

Gifts don't have to come just at the holidays.
You can give your existing and past clients gifts any time of the year—not just at Christmas time. There are numerous occasions where giving a gift would really make you stand out from the crowd. For example, give a gift or goodie when you receive a referral from a client, on the one-year anniversary of your working together, on or around Thanksgiving (use the holiday to thank them again for their business), as a thank you for spending a significant amount of money with you, or to celebrate their attracting a new client, etc.

How Would You Feel?

One of the reasons I teach solo small business owners to continually market to their existing and past clients is to help them avoid that feast-and-famine roller-coaster of an inconsistent client load that can be so common when your small business is you.

But, there is another *big* reason … by marketing to existing and past clients continually, and on a consistent basis, you prime them to turn to you again when they have another need for your services. You also stay in touch with them continually as a way to build an ongoing relationship with them, so that if things are ever slow and you have to pick up the phone to ask for more business or a referral to someone they think you can help, you don't look like "Johnny Come Lately".

Think about how you would feel if you worked with a small business owner, were satisfied with their service, would use them again in the future, but you never heard from them again—until one day you get a call from them saying something to the effect of, "Hi Jane, it's Tom. Things are kinda slow, and I just wanted to call and check in and see if I could help you with anything. No? Okay, do you know anyone else I could call?"

How would you feel? Probably unappreciated and maybe a bit taken advantage of. I know I would. Continually marketing to existing and past clients when you don't need the business will alleviate this. When you call, you can say, "As you know, I have been sending you my monthly newsletters (or monthly sales coupons or monthly tips sheets or whatever). I hope they have been helpful and have given you a lot of value. I wanted to call to follow up and see if there was anything else I could do for you?" If the response is "yes," fantastic, you've just made more money and kept a past client in the pipeline and happy. If the response is "no," you can rest assured that the "no" would be more of a "No, not right now, but if something comes up, I will definitely give you a call. In the meantime, why don't you call Bob," versus the "No, I don't need anything and, no, I don't know anyone else you can call," which is what happens when a past client doesn't hear from you for a long time.

A Final Word About Your Clients

Remember: without clients, you don't have a small business. Your clients are the means to living the life you want and generating the income you desire. They are literally your bread and butter. If you think about it, your clients have paid for your house, your car, your vacations—essentially, they've given you the money to have the things you have and to buy the things you've bought. Take care of those who have taken care of you. Don't forget them, remember where you came from. ◆

Avoid These Common Mistakes

You've no doubt heard the saying, "You learn from your mistakes." I believe it's true. I personally think I learn a lot more from my mistakes than I do from my successes (which is a little aggravating at times). Many others hold this same belief.

Common Marketing Mistakes

I see solo small business owners make a number of very common mistakes in their marketing. I hear the following statement almost weekly from solo small business owners: "I really don't know or understand why my marketing isn't working."

There are many possible reasons why your marketing isn't working. Let's take a look at ten of the biggies—ten common marketing mistakes that solo small business owners make. As you're reading this chapter, keep in mind what I taught you earlier—marketing is as much about image and the little things as it is about tools and activities. Hopefully, by my providing you with this list, you'll have an "a-ha" moment and be able to correct something you may have overlooked.

Common Mistake #1: Being a Lemming

A common mistake I see is what I call "marketing like a herd of lemmings." You know what lemmings are, don't you? They're animals that follow each other blindly; one lemming steps off a cliff and the rest all do the same.

Marketing like a herd of lemmings looks like this: Other businesses advertise in the yellow pages; you do too. Other businesses send out coupons in the mail; you do, too. Other businesses paper the suburbs with door hangers and flyers; you do, too. Other businesses advertise in the paper; you do, too.

What works for one business doesn't work for all. Marketing a service is different from marketing a product. And the way to market one service can be very different from the way you market another service. And marketing a solo small business is different too.

Remember the nail salon example? The young woman listening to my workshop was going to market her small business like a herd of lemmings—by advertising in the Yellow Pages, since every other retail business did.

Don't be a lemming. Just because "everyone else does it," does not mean that you should. Avoiding this mistake will save you a lot of wasted time and money.

Common Mistake #2: Sporadic Chaos

Don't get sucked into "the sporadic chaos of marketing." Most solo small businesses are sporadic in their marketing activities (which is closely related to the Marketing A.D.D. disease I talked about in Chapter 13). They just meander through the activities of marketing with no focused direction and no plan.

To be successful at marketing, you must have focus (focus, focus, focus) and have a plan. Most solo small businesses do not have either one. For most solo small businesses, the sporadic chaos of marketing goes something like this: You say to yourself, "I need to market myself." So you think, "I'll join a leads group." Then you think, "I should send out that sales letter." But, then you get distracted into thinking, "I should put together a postcard and mail it out." But, then there's the "My comprehensive, workhorse website really needs to be finished," "Oops, there's the phone," and "Hey, I got a nice, big, new client."

Then it turns into, "Wow, I'm busy and haven't marketed myself in months." Panic sets in as you think, "I have no business. I gotta get something going here." So you start with, "How about I call some old clients for a referral?" Then you realize, "I didn't get too much from that. How about that business after-hours social with the Chamber of Commerce?" But, you don't get much action, so you think, "I'll get a brochure printed and mail that out."

That sick feeling in your stomach intensifies as you realize, "Man, I don't want to cold call." "Oops, there's the phone again." You celebrate because it's Jeff from four months ago. He now wants to get started. You're truckin' along happily, since you think, "Wow, I am busy with Jeff's job." But then the panic starts to creep up, "Yikes! Jeff's job is almost done, and I have no more work. I need more clients." And on and on and on and on we go; where you stop, nobody knows. The vicious cycle continues.

Avoid sporadic chaos; remember what you have learned. Pick a niche. Choose between three and six marketing tools to strategically diversify your efforts. Test and tweak. Focus, focus, focus. Then lather, rinse and repeat consistently over the long-haul.

No more sporadic chaos—just focused efforts.

Common Mistake #3: Not Spending Any Money

A big mistake is not spending any money on marketing yourself. Oh, I know, I know—your a solo small business. You have no money. Join the crowd; everyone tells me that. I understand. It's the same for most solo small business owners. The same was true when I started my solo small business.

Bottom line: if you're in business and want to stay in business, you must find a marketing budget somewhere. You have to spend money to make money. We've all heard that, and it's true. Marketing doesn't work if you don't spend any money, or if you're suffering from not-spending-any-money's second cousin—the mindset that you can't afford it.

I'm sorry to be blunt, but you *must* afford it.

If you will stop focusing on how you *can't* afford something or how much money you *don't* have, which is a "poverty mentality," and focus on *having* money and *being able* to afford things, which is a "rich mentality," you will be much more successful!

This one little shift makes a world of difference. I have seen so many solo small business owners completely turn their business around and become completely swamped with work and more clients than they could handle, by just changing their attitude and mindset to one of "I will spend money to make money, and I will find a way to afford this. I do have money, I can afford things …."

It's amazing, really. When you accept the reality that you must spend money to make money, you stop being a victim of money and start to be its master. You change the "I don'ts" to "I wills." It's a very powerful shift.

Common Mistake #4: Do-It-Yourself Plastic Surgery

I'd like you to imagine for a moment that you wake up one morning, look in the mirror and say to yourself, "You know, I am just not as good looking as I think I should be. I'm going to have some plastic surgery done. But wait, plastic surgery is very expensive and I am a self-employed solo small business owner with limited funds. So, to save money, I'll just do it myself. Barnes and Noble® has a book on plastic surgery. I'll buy the book and do it myself."

So, you go to Barnes and Noble, buy a book on plastic surgery, read it, pull a sharp knife out of your kitchen drawer and go to work hacking away at your face. You wanted to save some money, so the do-it-yourself route seemed the best choice. Sounds ludicrous, doesn't it? You would never do plastic surgery on yourself. But that's exactly what you're doing if you do your own graphic design, website design or marketing when you're not a graphic designer, website designer or professional marketer.

You're hacking away at your image, which is just like hacking away at your face. You are killing the image and professionalism of your business.

Too many small businesses use the do-it-yourself approach to graphic design for their business. It's a huge mistake you cannot afford to make. Unless you are a professional graphic designer—meaning you are professionally trained in graphic design, and your full-time profession, not a hobby, is graphic design—then you have no business doing the graphic design work for your small business.

Unfortunately, most small business owners just don't get this. They don't realize how costly the mistake of designing their own marketing materials truly is—and by marketing materials I mean absolutely everything that comes from your small business, from your logo to your business card to your website to your brochures and flyers. If you design the marketing materials for your solo small business and you are not a professional, you are damaging your business.

What's the Big Deal?

By doing your own graphic design, you're creating a sub-par first impression that will be burned into the mind of new prospects forever. You'll never get a second chance to make a first impression.

As a solo small business, you cannot afford to look thrown together, cheap and unprofessional, which is exactly how you'll look if you do your own "plastic surgery."

Doing-It-Yourself Can Be a Costly Mistake

This mistake is very costly for one simple reason: too many small businesses look alike. Too many look cheap. Too many look unprofessional. Most, in an attempt to save money, just throw their marketing materials together or hire the cheapest person they can find to design them.

If you do this, you will look like the thousands of other small businesses that have done the same. You won't stand out from the crowd. You won't look like the expert that you are, and you won't attract good-paying clients. You'll attract the prospects looking for the cheapest, because that's what you look like—and that is precisely why this mistake is so costly.

Don't make this huge mistake of do-it-yourself plastic surgery. Stand out from the crowd. Be different. Look different. If you don't stand out, if you don't look professional, if you look cheap, amateurish and thrown-together, a few things will happen:

➤ Your services will be passed over, and the prospect will go to a competitor.
➤ You will not be paid the price you are worth.
➤ You will not be trusted as the very best in your field.
➤ You will be seen and judged as something you are not.

➤ You will have a hard time building your reputation.

➤ And, most of all, you will lose money.

The Remedy

The only way to stand out from the overcrowded market-place and correct this mistake is to have a professional, reputable graphic designer create and produce all of your marketing materials. Having these materials professionally created is an investment, not an expense. Professionally designed materials brand you as the expert you are, attract clients to your business and position your business above your competition.

Don't make the same mistake so many other small business owners make. Hire a professional. Do it right the first time. A professional image will put you light-years ahead of your competition. You will stand out from your competition and project the image of your expertise. This is an investment that will pay for itself time and time again for the life of your business.

Even if You're in the Design Industry ...

For those of you in the design world who read this book—the architects, interior designers, web designers and other graphic designers—you, too, need to seriously consider hiring an outside designer for your materials.

Why in the world do I suggest you do this? Because you're way too close to your own business to design your own materials. I don't care if you are the next kick-butt, award-winning Frank Lloyd Wright, don't do your own design. There's a reason why doctors don't operate on themselves or their relatives. There's a reason why lawyers don't represent themselves in court. There's a reason why designers should not design for your own businesses—you're just too close.

Common Mistake #5: Taking Referrals Lightly

I referred a fellow colleague to a great client of mine. Did my colleague pick up the phone and follow up on that referral immediately, or did he wait a week, two weeks, three weeks to call? You guessed it. Three weeks later, my colleague still hadn't called the client. I asked him, "Did you call John?" The answer was, "Not yet, I have just been so busy."

Let me pause a minute and go bang my head against the wall. What was my colleague thinking? This was a hot referral—almost guaranteed business. Your fingers should be dialing while I am giving you the information. But no, he didn't. Sale lost. I look dumb.

Never, never, treat a referral as just another lead. Hello! Referrals are gifts. Don't take them for granted. The fact that you received a referral means that someone values what you do. Someone cares enough about you and thinks you can do a good job, so much so that they will send a friend, associate, family member or colleague to you.

You'd darn well better immediately call that referral and do your very best to meet their needs. If you do get the job, work your tail off doing the best you can do, update the person who gave you the referral on how it is going and thank them for giving you the referral.

Referrals are never automatic; they are a gift. 99% of solo small business owners rely on referrals as a huge chunk of their client base. Failure to treat referrals with the utmost importance and care is saying, "I don't really care if you give me referrals, because I don't handle them immediately." Is that the marketing message you want to send?

Common Mistake #6: Being Afraid to Admit Your Mistakes and Correct Them

As a marketing consultant, author, speaker and designer, I sometimes have to rely on outside vendors to fulfill some of the projects for my clients. Those outside vendors have the ability to make me look really good to my clients, or really bad. If a vendor does something wrong or screws something up, it can be okay—as long as they apologize, fix the mistake and really make it up to the client. If they don't, then I'm gone—and I'll never use that vendor again.

Case in point: I recently decided to work with a new vendor. This vendor was highly recommended to me by someone I know and trust—a colleague of mine who is the consummate professional. The vendor raved to me about their quality, prices and customer service. They assured me that they would go above and beyond the call of duty and that my clients and I would be well taken care of.

Then the work began … missed deadlines, inaccurate billing and no follow-up on delivery time. I was madder than—well, you know.

This vendor promised me and my client one thing and did something completely different. This vendor quoted me and my client one price, then charged another. This vendor gave me and my client a deadline and completely missed it.

I have two words for this vendor: "See ya!"

This vendor made me look stupid to my client, since I was the one who suggested to my client that we use the vendor. This is a very big sin to commit as a vendor, when your paycheck depends on service providers like me to bring you clients. To make it worse, *I* had to approach the vendor and ask them to fix the problems. They didn't so much as volunteer.

Needless to say, I will never ever use that vendor again. Period.

We all make mistakes. It's going to happen—we're human. The difference between being a trustworthy professional and a flake is how you handle your mistakes. When you make a mistake, be the person who calls and apologizes. Don't run and hide. Don't avoid the situation. Be a professional. Call the client and apologize and do something to rectify the situation. Give a discount, offer another service, give a gift as a way to say you're sorry, or at the very least, write an apology note.

More times than not, a person just wants to hear, "I'm sorry. I messed up, and here is what I am going to do to fix it." If you own up to your mistake and fix the problem, chances are, you'll keep the client.

Common Mistake #7: Expecting Instant Gratification

I discussed in Chapter 12 the idea that marketing is a long-term relationship, not a one-shot deal. Marketing takes time. A common mistake that many solo small business owners make is wanting and even expecting instant gratification from all of their marketing activities.

You join a referral group and expect a pile of referrals the first meeting you attend. You launch a website and expect a flood of traffic within the first few weeks, etc. More times than not, marketing doesn't work this way. Sure, you may launch a marketing campaign and generate great results instantly: but if you make this your common expectation, you will be disappointed.

Marketing is a long-term relationship that is to be nurtured and cared for over the long haul. Marketing is not an event—it's a continual process.

If you eradicate from your mind the want and need for instant gratification in your marketing efforts … the marketing you do for your solo small business will not only be much more successful, but much more enjoyable.

Common Mistake #8: Not Marketing Soon Enough

You undoubtedly know by now that marketing takes time, and results usually don't come immediately. Unfortunately, many solo small business owners forget this fact, which is why they commit the all-too-common mistake of not marketing soon enough.

Not marketing soon enough looks like this: waiting until your pipeline has completely dried up and you desperately need clients before you conduct any marketing activities. If you wait until you have no business and your pipeline is dry … you have waited too long. It's too late. You will have a very tough road ahead of you.

You have to start marketing sooner, rather than later. You need to market yourself before you even *think* you need to market yourself.

Marketing takes time. When you start a marketing activity, there will be some lag-time between the date you start marketing and the date you get a new client. Marketing ahead of time will dramatically decrease this lag-time.

By not marketing soon enough, you'll approach marketing from a need or panic mindset. Whether you're conscious of this mindset or not—it will happen. No one wants to work with someone who is needy and when you need clients it will be very hard not to be, well, needy. You *need* clients. You *need* to market yourself. Needy, needy, needy. There is a very strange phenomenon that occurs when one is in a place of need: it seems the needier you are, the less you will attract. You may have experienced this before—when you need clients, you can't seem to attract them. When you don't need clients, you can't seem to turn them away.

Don't make this common mistake. Start marketing now—right now—before you're put in the position of having to play catch-up. The sooner you start your marketing, the better.

Common Mistake #9: Sending Out Something Once and Expecting Results

I'm not going to go into much detail about this common mistake since I have already spent a lot of time discussing how imperative it is to market again and again and again. Hopefully, by now, you know and understand why this is a big no-no.

I've listed this mistake one last time as a reminder. The interesting thing is that I see a lot of small business owners making this mistake, but they don't even realize it. This mistake is so common (in fact, I think it may very well be the *most* common) that it gets missed. So here it is once again in black and white: if you find yourself struggling with marketing, the first place to check yourself is to make sure you're not just sending out something once and expecting it to work.

Common Mistake #10: Marketing Only When You Have the Time

I see a lot of solo small business owners caught in what I call the "feast- and-famine roller-coaster of inconsistent marketing." The reason: they market their small business *only* when they have the time.

When your small business is you, you do it all—run your small business, market your small business, work with your clients—the list goes on and on. What inevitably happens is, you get busy—really busy—and nine times out of ten you don't have time, or worse yet, you don't take time to market your services.

Sound familiar?

I see this happen all the time. Not a week goes by that I don't talk to a solo small business owner who says, "Wow, I am really, really busy. Business is booming," to which I reply, "That's great! Congratulations! Are you still marketing in the midst of being busy?" I cannot remember *ever* hearing someone say "yes."

The fact is, you must market your small business when you have the time and when you don't have the time. Bottom line—market *all* the time.

Take out your calendar and make yourself an appointment each and every single week to work on and conduct three to six strategically diversified marketing activities and tools. Do this every single week. Make it a firm appointment that you cannot miss.

Solo small business owners who market themselves all the time are the ones who are the most successful. They are also less stressed out, simply because they are not running around in a panic, feeling sick to their stomachs by continuing to ride the feast-and-famine roller-coaster of inconsistent marketing. They have a full client load. They have a full pipeline. Do you want the same for your small business? Market all the time, and you will. Market both when you have time and when you don't!

These are just ten of the most common mistakes I see solo small business owners run into all the time. Avoid them, and you'll be light-years ahead of your competition.

There are quite a few more marketing mistakes that I see solo small business owners make. To find out what they are and how to fix them, be sure and visit www.MarketingForSolos.com and request your free copy of my audio program and workbook: "7 Deadly Marketing Mistakes That Can Bankrupt Your Solo Small Business and How To Erradicate Them Forever." ◆

—

16

Answers to Your Questions

Here are answers to a few good questions I have been asked over the years while speaking, teaching bootcamps and workshops. I know they can help you and your solo small business succeed. Of course, I do not have room in this book to answer all of the questions I receive. If you have a question that I can help you with, see the end of this chapter for my contact information.

Question:

I'm just starting out and have a very limited budget. If I can only choose one marketing activity, what should it be?

Answer:

I am going to make an assumption that you have or will have a professional logo and stationery package designed. This is a given and the very first place to start. Now, I never, ever suggest that solos only do one marketing activity. One is a very dangerous number (due to everything I discussed in Chapter 7). But, let's assume that you really have no money at all. If that's the case, once you have your logo and stationery in place, I highly recommend doing two marketing activities. The first would be to make yourself as visible as humanly possible. Attend every single networking function you can, give demonstrations, open houses, free trials, etc. Do anything you can to make yourself more visible. Second would be to join a formal, structured referral group, such as BNI, or one of the others listed in the Appendix section of this book. Once you begin to get clients, you need to move to the three to six strategically diversified marketing tools and activities that we discussed in Chapter 8 as soon as possible!

Question:

I am overwhelmed with options. Where do I start?

Answer:

It's very common, as a solo small business owner, to be overwhelmed at the seemingly endless marketing opportunities and possibilities. Did you see the graphic on Page 70? No wonder overwhelm can be a problem. Start by deciding exactly what target you want to focus on—what niche you will go after. Once you do this, you will be able to pick three to six strategic marketing activities to focus on that will best reach your chosen niche. Remember to focus, focus, focus, and you won't be scattered about trying a million different things to reach a million different people. And remember to test, because the first three to six you choose may not be the ones you do forever. The important thing is to just choose and get started! Then you can tweak and adjust things.

Question:

What is the best form of marketing for my type of business? Everyone seems to have an opinion about what has worked for them, but it never seems to work for me.

Answer:

Marketing a service-based business is very different from marketing a product. Don't listen to everyone else's opinion. Follow what you have learned in this book ... remember this is the foundation of the Marketing for Solos® System™ ... a proven system that works! The tools and activities discussed in Chapter 8 are proven methods that work for small, one-person, service-based businesses. When you pick three to six of those tools to strategically diversify and focus your efforts over the long haul, you will get results. Something in your question makes me sense that you may be looking for that "magic bullet," that one thing that will serve all your marketing needs. You may have tried a little bit of everything looking for the magic bullet. Marketing doesn't work that way. Pick your three to six tools and activities and focus on them. The magic bullet is the combination of all of the principles you've learned about in this book.

Question:

How do you find the best demographic to target?

Answer:

As you learned in Chapter 4, you need to pick a niche and focus on that niche. By doing so, you will become known as the expert for that niche, and people will seek you out and flock to you. There are two ways to pick a niche. One is to look at your current and past clients to see if there are any trends you can identify that may lead you to the right niche to focus on. The other way is to find something or some client group that you are passionate about and make that your focus. Every small business owner is different. We all have unique personalities, likes, dislikes and passions. Just because one demographic is profitable for one person does not mean it will be profitable for you. If you have a passion about a particular group of people and decide to focus your efforts in service to that group, you will most likely be profitable, because you will become well known for that group.

Now remember, as I mentioned before: the niche you choose must follow three criteria:

1. The niche must have a history of purchasing the service or services you're offering.
2. The niche must be easy to find and market to.
3. The niche must be large enough to sustain you.

There are no hard and fast rules for how many people have to be in a niche for it to be big enough. It is sometimes a best judgment call. Try the niche out, see how it works. If you come up with too few prospects, widen the niche a bit. The main thing is to focus. Just get in there, pick a niche and get focused. One last thing about niches: you must pick a niche that you are passionate about, not just one that will make you a lot of money. If you are just focusing on a niche for the money, people will see this coming a mile away. Pick a niche that you truly believe in, are passionate about and want to work with.

Question:

What's the easiest, most affordable and most effective way for a new solo small business owner to market themselves?

Answer:

Three things:

1. Find a niche to focus on. This will attract clients to you much faster than trying to focus on the "anyone, everyone and someone" approach.
2. Be very, very visible. Attend every single net-working event you possibly can. These are usually quite affordable. As a new small business owner, you have to get the word out that you are in business.
3. Get involved in a formal referral organization such as BNI or one of the others that I list in the Appendix.

Question:

If I am going to do a direct mail campaign, what is the best way to follow-up? Should I limit the number of people on the list so I'll actually have time to call them? If I choose to do a higher number of mailings, does this prevent me from being able to do any follow-up?

Answer:

This is a very good question. If you are planning a direct mail campaign and you want to call the prospect after the mailing to follow up with them, then yes, you will need to limit the number of pieces you mail. You also need to be very careful about "no call" or "no solicitation" laws in your state. Make sure you're not calling someone on a "do not call" list, or you can get into a lot of trouble. The first and most important element in a successful direct mail campaign is the mailing list. Make sure you have a finely tuned, highly targeted list. Also remember that, even if you are going to call the list and follow up, they will still need to see your message time and time again (six times as the bare minimum). You may want to schedule your campaign with a mailing, then a call, then another mailing or two and another call, then another few mailings with a final call at the end. This way, your audience will get to know you over the long haul on two marketing fronts: your mailings and your follow-up calls.

Question:

I work as an independent professional for a very large corporation that is highly regulated. I am now a solo small business, but the services I sell are from a large corporation. The company wants us to market our businesses through referrals and a warm market, not advertising-related methods. The problem is, I am relatively new and don't have a warm market, so what do I do?

Answer:

Even if you are selling the services provided by a large corporation, your solo small business is you; therefore, you have to market you and the solutions to the pain, problem or predicament of your prospects. If the large company does not want you to market yourself with anything but referrals, you can still be very successful. The key is—you can probably guess what I am about to say—picking a niche and focusing on that niche. Anyone can pick a niche. No matter if you are an insurance agent representing a large company or a financial planner representing a large company, you still need to find a niche to focus on. Then, when you are attending all of the networking events and referral groups to generate those referrals, people will know your focus and can more accurately and comfortably refer you to clients.

I recently had coffee with a friend of mine who is an insurance agent. During our meeting, we discussed this very topic. He sells property and casualty insurance (auto, home and life insurance), for a big company. As you well know, this is an extremely competitive industry. My friend and I were trying to figure out a niche that he could focus on. Well, he loves motorcycles. He owns several and rides every single chance he has. It just so happened that his company had a great motorcycle policy, so he decided motorcycle owners would be the niche he'd focus on. He mentioned that he would be able to network with fellow motorcycle owners in riding groups, and he could do some joint ventures and networking with the local motorcycle dealerships in town. These are great ideas, and I'm confident that my insurance agent friend will achieve great results from his efforts. He didn't let the fact he's an agent for a big national company keep him from picking a niche—and you shouldn't either. Bottom line: don't let the big company with big regulations stop you from picking a niche and focusing your efforts to that audience. You will get results by doing so. You will develop a name for yourself in that niche and your marketing—even though regulated by the big company—will be much easier.

Question:

If I need business today—I mean actually this minute, today—I have to get a client right now. How do I do that?

Answer:

First, you should never, ever put yourself in a position of needing business right now, today, this very minute. You may be in this position because you made common mistake #8: not marketing soon enough, or common mistake #10: marketing only when you have the time. Both of these are discussed in Chapter 15. Consistently marketing yourself over and over and over, when you need clients and when you don't, will prevent this from happening. Even if you are brand new in business, you should have a little bit of money saved to get started, because it will take time to generate your first client. But, let's assume that you have done everything right. You have consistently marketed yourself, and you still need a client right now. I would suggest that you get on the phone and call all of your past clients. Approach them from a *giving* mentality, not a *getting* mentality. Ask if there is anything else you can do for them or if you can help them out in any way. Then you can ask them if they know someone you can help. *Only* after you have offered to help them can you ask them to help you. If you go through your entire client list, you should be able to receive at least one referral. Then get on the phone and call them. After you have exhausted this measure, go back through all of the prospects you talked to in the past who said, "Call me later." Follow up with all of those contacts. Make sure that you have, indeed, followed up on every single contact and prospect and that they are, in fact a "no." You will be very surprised that sometimes following up with a prospect who you thought, "Well this one is cold: I know they won't buy from me," will, in fact, remember you and may buy from you. But, you will never know until you try.

I hope these questions and answers help you in your solo small business marketing. These are by no means, all of the questions you'll have, but they should help you. If you have a question not answered here, be sure and visit my website at:

www.MarketingForSolos.com

And if you'd like a way to get all of your marketing questions answered on a monthly basis, check out the Marketing for Solos® Academy program. In addition to receiving personal guidance, mentoring, teaching, resources and accountability to keep you plugged in and motivated, as you market your services successfully, you'll also have access to monthly Q&A calls, where you can get answers to *any* marketing question you have. Visit: www.MarketingFor SolosAcademy.com for details. ◆

The Final Review

Whew! You made it. You're at the end of the book and ready to put everything you've learned into practice. Many solo small business owners fail at marketing because they do not focus, focus, focus and have a plan—a first, second, third, fourth and fifth step. This won't be the case for you because in your hands is a system for marketing. The Marketing for Solos® System™ and it is proven.

Here is a final review of all the steps involved in marketing your solo small business successfully.

The Cold, Hard Truth

First, remember: No one cares about you—they only care about themselves. You have to market to your prospects' needs and desires, not your own.

Change Your Thinking

Next, change your thinking. In all of your marketing activities, focus first on the client and their 3Ps—pain, problem, predicament—not on yourself and your needs. Give to receive.

Find Your Niche and You'll Get Rich

Then, find your niche. Make sure it's one you're passionate about. Focus on that niche and keep working it.

Speak the Language of Results

Once you have your niche, you must speak in the language of your prospects: put their needs first. Answer the big question: "What's in it for me?" which can also be stated as: what they get, why they should care, and why they should trust and hire you. Speak to their pain, problem or predicament. Speak to their emotions. Avoid labels.

Deliver Your Message

The two most powerful tools to focus and deliver the most effective message are the Situation/Solution Summary™ and the "What Do You Do?" Commercial™.

Market LESS To Be More Successful

Apply the principle of Strategic Diversification to your marketing and choose three to six doable, manageable, repeatable tools and activities. Avoid the sporadic chaos of marketing by focusing on those activities only.

Choose the Right Tools

Chapter 8 is filled with proven tools and activities that will help you successfully market your business. Choose three to six of them and use them consistently.

Hire Marketing Help

Spend your time on the things that you are qualified to do and are passionate about. Hire a graphic designer to design a professional look for your company. Hire a website designer for your website and a marketing consultant or coach to help you, as well.

Sometimes It's the Little Things

Always be aware of the image you project in your marketing materials, in your speech, in your actions and in your demeanor. Treat your clients well, and always be professional in the big and little things.

Testing, Testing, Is This Thing On?

Testing is important, and it works. Always test your marketing activities, and be ready to tweak them and test again. The easiest way to test is to ask clients and others what they think. Chapter 11 has additional tools for testing.

Lather, Rinse, Repeat

Marketing is a process, not a one-shot deal. You need to repeat your marketing activities at least once a month for six months. Twelve months or more is better.

Be Consistent

Consistency is the mark of the professional. Be consistent in your image and in your activities. Consistently market yourself, even when you're busy.

Remember Where You Came From

Existing and past clients are the clients who have gotten you where you are today. Don't forget about them. Don't take them for granted. Stay in touch with them. Continue to build the relationship. Continually show them how much you appreciate their business, or they will go elsewhere.

Avoid Common Mistakes

Avoid the common marketing mistakes that solo small business owner often make.

Go Forth and Prosper!

Your company isn't going to market itself. Get out there and get going. Now!

You've got all of the proven tools, techniques, strategies and tactics to market your solo small business successfully. How successful you are is up to one person—you. ◆

CHAPTER

Go Forth and Prosper!

I absolutely love the Nike® slogan "Just Do It." Yeah, it's been around for awhile, but it's so poignant and says so much in three little words. So, borrowing Nike's slogan, I want to tell you it's time to "Just Do It!"

It's Time for Action

It's time for you to start. That's it. Go. Start. Do it. We're at the end of the book, and it is time for you to start marketing yourself and never, ever quit.

I have been preaching throughout this book that marketing is not an event, it's a long-term commitment. You don't just do marketing, you commit to it. You do it for the rest of your solo small business' life.

Don't Do What Others Do, Which is Usually Nothing

Do something. Do it now. You've read this book. You have the tools. You have the knowledge and techniques. Now, get out there and do it.

Unfortunately, way too many solo small business owners don't do anything. They read book after book after book and go to seminar after seminar, but they don't do anything with all of the knowledge they gain. Seems like a waste, doesn't it?

Maybe you're afraid of failure. Don't be. You have guarded against that by educating yourself in the proven techniques and system for marketing a solo small business. It's only when you fail to act on the knowledge you have that you fail.

Some Things to Watch For ...

There are a few tendencies that some solo small business owners have when it comes to actually getting out there and marketing themselves. If you notice yourself doing these things, stop. Regroup. Get moving and keep going!

➤ Don't get so overwhelmed by the marketing possibilities and choices that you freeze and do nothing. Review what you have learned. Pick the niche you'll focus on. Pick the three to six activities to strategically diversify your efforts, and commit to the long-haul.

➤ There's a tendency for solo small business owners to want to wait until everything is perfect in life and in business before they get started. Don't wait. Start marketing now. If you wait until everything is perfect, you'll be waiting forever.

➤ Don't wait for or expect perfection. Remember: nothing will ever be perfect. Your comprehensive, workhorse website will never be perfect That's okay, get it done and keep tweaking and adding information. Your "What Do You Do?" Commercial™ will never be perfect. So what? Use what you have and continue to work on it until it gets better and more effective. Your mailings will never be perfect. Get them out there and begin building your repetition and momentum in the marketplace. Remember, you will be testing and tweaking to make them better.

➤ Don't wait. The point here is get moving today. Quit waiting or hiding in your office. Quit thinking, "I am so overwhelmed I don't know where to start." Just start.

This book has given you the system for standing out from the crowd and attracting clients consistently, but they will only work if you take the information and put it into practice. You have absolutely nothing to lose and a lot to gain—more clients and better income.

One Final Thought to Send You on Your Way

As I close this book, I want to leave you with one final thought. I share this with you as a personal story to encourage you as you market your solo small business successfully.

On my desk, I have a paperweight with a quote from Winston Churchill that says, "Never, never, never quit". I also have an old Chinese proverb taped to my computer monitor that says, "The temptation to quit will be greatest just before you're about to succeed."

So, why I am I telling you this? Because, at some point in your solo small business career, you are going to want to quit. You're going to want to throw in the towel and exclaim, "ENOUGH! I've had it! I'm going back to the comforts of corporate America or a real job."

Don't. Don't you dare quit. Bite, scratch, claw and do whatever necessary to make it as a solo small business owner. The benefits far outweigh the negatives. They really do. If they didn't, one in every three Americans would not venture out on their own as new small business owners.

I can predict and tell you right here and now what will happen in your solo small business. Obviously, you must market yourself to get clients. This is not optional. It's why you're reading this book. It's why you bought it. You must succeed in marketing.

But, here's what going to happen—I guarantee it. You will do everything right. You will find a niche to focus on. You will start focusing on the prospect first. You will speak the language of results. You will answer the prospects' big questions of, "What's in it for me?" You will choose three to six marketing tools and activities to strategically diversify your efforts. You will test your efforts and tweak things until they work. You will market yourself consistently and repeatedly. And, you will remember where you came from.

But, at some point after doing all of this, at some point of doing everything right, you will want to quit. Business will slow down or come to a standstill. This whole "marketing thing" will seem to not be working. You may even curse the ground I walk on for teaching you to market consistently over and over and over again. "Great, Jeanna!" you'll shout. "Yeah, if over and over and over again works and you know what you're talking about, then why, at this particular moment do I not have clients?"

My answer to you would be: never, never, never quit. Period. Because, my fellow solo small business owner friend, this "marketing stuff" *does* work. This Marketing for Solos® System™ *does* work. It is proven. Very successful solo small businesses market themselves this way and thrive. I do for my own solo small business and you can, too. It does work, but it ONLY works if you never, never, never quit.

Let me give you a real life example from me, in my own life. In the middle of writing this book, I had one heck of a three day span over the course of one week.

I woke up on Monday and thought, "What's the point? Why am I doing this? I am a successful marketing consultant and designer. I market my solo small business exactly the way I teach my clients to market their solo small business. I market my services consistently, over and over and over again. Even when I am slammed with business, I am still out there marketing. But, what's the point?" I continued to ask myself.

You see, that Monday was just another Monday in a long string of what seemed like forever with no new clients. I had gone about four weeks without signing one single new client, which for my solo small business is very, very rare and a definite huge dry spell.

I was marketing myself consistently. Every single week I was actively marketing. I promise you, I absolutely practice what I preach. But still, nothing.

I started to get that low-grade almost panic of the internal voice saying, "Hello, I have bills to pay. I have a car payment. I need clients in order to eat. Hello, why isn't this marketing thing working?"

Tuesday was even worse.

The voices in my head were going crazy. Just about then I made the "mistake" of going to the mailbox to check my mail. Oh, great, four big bills to pay. Yippee! I am so glad that I have no new clients.

But then Wednesday completely turned the week around. It's almost as if God whacked me upside the head and said, "Duh, Jeanna. Never, never, never quit."

Wednesday morning is my BNI group. When the time came to pass referrals, I received two—both of them to design and create comprehensive, workhorse websites. These referrals were done deals, new clients ready to do business. It was simply a matter of signing the contracts.

Then, on the way back to my office, I checked my voicemail. One voicemail said, "Hi, Jeanna, this is ___. I was referred to you by ___. I have looked at your website and I'm ready to sign up for your Marketing for Solos® Marketing Mentoring Groups program." The second voicemail said, "Hi, Jeanna, this is ___. I was at the workshop you gave last week. I heard every word you said and I want to hire you for marketing help. Call me so we can set up a time to get started."

Holy cow! Four new clients in a matter of hours! But it gets even better. After I got back to my office and finalized everything with the two blazing hot referrals and set up appointments for the two new clients that hired me via voice mail, I got one more call. It was from a prospect whom I'd spoken with over a year ago. He called and said, "Okay, Jeanna, I have taken enough time on the fence. I know I need help. I am ready to hire you for the marketing project we talked about last May."

I hung up the phone and had to sit down to keep from falling down. Five clients in less than three hours. Yeah, this "marketing stuff" really works! That is, if you follow the proven strategies in this book and never, never, never quit!

Here I was doing everything right, doing every single thing that I have taught you to do, but not seeing the *immediate* results from my efforts (Hmm, was I expecting instant gratification?). I was ready to quit. But, I didn't quit. I never, never, never, ever quit, because my temptation to quit was greatest right before I succeeded—five clients in less than three hours.

And, my friend, this will, at some point, happen to you. It's life. We're human. In fact, you may have already experienced it. You will do everything right. You will find a niche to focus on. You will start focusing on the prospect first. You will speak the language of results. You will answer the prospect's big questions. You will choose three to six marketing tools and activities to strategically diversify and focus your efforts. And you will hit a dry spell. And you'll want to quit.

But again, I tell you, never, never, never quit.

C. J. Hayden in her book, *Get Clients Now!: A 28-Day Marketing Program for Professionals and Consultants,* says:

> "There is an interesting phenomenon that occurs when you get serious about marketing in a focused, consistent way. You begin to get results in unexpected places. The telephone rings and it's a prospect you spoke to three months ago saying he is suddenly interested in working with you. You go to a networking meeting that seems like a complete waste of time while you are there, and run into a hot new prospect in the elevator on your way out. You get an exciting referral from someone whose name you don't even recognize. It's almost as if the universe has noticed how hard you are working and decided to reward you." [6]

I couldn't agree more. Never, never, never quit.

When you do everything you should, when you put into practice the proven system that you have learned in this book, I promise, you WILL attract clients consistently.

Oh, one more thing. That day, that same Wednesday that I got five clients in less than three hours, as I was packing up to leave my office for the day, my phone rang. It was another prospect, who said,

6   C.J. Hayden, *Get Clients Now!: A 28-Day Marketing Program for Professionals and Consultants* (New York, NY: AMACOM, an imprint of AMA Publications, 1999). Pages 65-66.

"Hey, Jeanna, this is ____ from ____. Remember me? Well, I'm finally ready. I want to hire you to help market the new venture I have been talking about. What does your schedule look like the rest of this week?"

Make that six new clients in one business day ...

I wish you much success! ◆

About the Author

Jeanna Pool is a rare breed, in that she's an expert in both marketing that actually works and graphic design that actually sells … two disciplines and competencies that very, very few can bring together successfully.

Born and raised in Odessa, Texas (she graduated from the same high school featured in the movie Friday Night Lights) she is the only child of two very successful, entrepreneurial parents. Jeanna was conditioned from birth that she, too, would someday own her own solo small business. Forget about her wanting to become an astronaut; entrepreneur was her only option.

Before striking out on her own, she worked as a graphic designer, website designer and marketing specialist for a variety of firms and a variety of clients in a variety of industries—everything from corporate America to non-profits to government.

Today Jeanna owns and operates Marketing for Solos® which is her own, highly successful, award-winning, solo small business. She works exclusively with solo small business owners all across the United States, Canada, Europe, Australia and around the world. All of Jeanna's clients have one thing in common—they are really good at what they do, but sometimes really struggle to market their services successfully and balance life as a solo.

Jeanna has been called one of the world's foremost experts on marketing a one-person small business. Her love and passion is helping other solo small business owners be as outrageously successful as they possibly can be. Her no-nonsense, straightforward, passionate, motivational, fun-loving personality shines through in all of the marketing coaching, mentoring, training and work she does for her clients. Jeanna lives, works and plays in Denver, Colorado.

More Information

The author, Jeanna Pool, is available for speaking engagements, keynote addresses, as well as, teaching workshops, seminars and break-out sessions for groups and associations, public seminars, events and industry-specific trainings. Through her dynamic, motivational, fun-loving, information filled presentations, Jeanna draws on her personal experiences and years of success in her own solo small business to share with audiences the essential elements and strategies to help them be as successful as they possibly can be in their solo small business marketing efforts. For more information or booking inquires, please call 303-380-9100 ext. 2 or send an email to: Speaking@MarketingForSolos.com. Jeanna is also available for a limited number of private consulting assignments. Visit the services section of the Marketing for Solos® website, located at: www.Marketing ForSolos.com/services for more information.

FREE Gift From The Author

Over **$497** In Marketing Tools and Resources Yours **FREE!**

As a very special thank you for purchasing this book, Jeanna Pool has a gift for you … a collection of valuable marketing tools, strategies and resources. Together, these normally sell for over $497, but as an owner of this book, they're yours absolutely free! To get your free gift simply visit: www.MarketingFor Solos.com/book-gift and follow the instructions.

BONUS ONE

FREE
Marketing Piece
Critique

This certificate entitles the owner of this book to submit *one* printed marketing piece—brochure, direct-mail letter or postcard, business card, flyer, or other similar marketing piece via postal mail for a free marketing critique by Jeanna Pool*.

Your Name: _____

Address: _____

City, State, Zip: _____

Phone: _____ Fax: _____

Email: _____

Send this certificate and your *one* marketing piece to:
Jeanna Pool
P.O. Box 460114
Denver, Colorado 80246

*TERMS: All material must be submitted via postal mail. Do not phone or email for critique. Critique will be supplied to you via fax or email only. Allow 8-12 weeks for response. Actual finished, printed materials, photocopies or a rough sketch may be submitted. Submitted materials will NOT be returned. If more than one item is submitted, only one critique of one item will be supplied. Please note, by submitting this form, you give Jeanna Pool permission to publish the marketing piece you supply and her critique in any of her books or publications, including her websites, as examples, without any compensation (monetary or otherwise).

BONUS TWO

FREE
Marketing Suggestion
and Feedback

This certificate entitles the owner of this book to briefly describe your biggest marketing challenge or question, and Jeanna Pool will respond with a suggestion and feedback*.

Biggest marketing challenge or question: _____

_____

_____

_____

_____

Your Name: _____

Address: _____

City, State, Zip: _____

Phone: _____ Fax: _____

Email: _____

Send this certificate to:
Jeanna Pool
P.O. Box 460114
Denver, Colorado 80246

*TERMS: This certificate must be submitted via postal mail. Do not phone or email for feedback. Feedback will be supplied to you via fax or email only. Allow 8-12 weeks for response. You may attach one separate sheet if necessary to this certificate for the description of your marketing challenge. Please note, by submitting this form, you give Jeanna Pool permission to publish your challenge/question and her suggestion/feedback in any of her books or publications, including her websites, as examples, without any compensation (monetary or otherwise).

APPENDIX A

Resources

Additional Resources from Jeanna Pool

Jeanna Pool Works With Solo Small Business Owners In Three Ways:

1. For the "Do-It-Yourself" Type of Solo ...

Jeanna has an entire catalog of books, training materials, products and resources all geared to help you create and implement the best marketing tools and activities for your solo small business. These materials are perfect for when you want to know how to do-it-all-by-yourself (the right way) and generate stellar results from all of your marketing efforts.

Here are just a few of the topics Jeanna covers in her books, training materials, products and resources ...

- Article Marketing
- Brochures and Collateral Materials
- Building Your Email List and Prospect List
- Comprehensive, Workhorse Website™
- Direct Mail
- Niche Marketing
- Online Marketing
- Postcard Marketing
- Press Releases
- Search Engine Optimization
- Social Media Marketing
- Video Marketing
- What Do You Do? Commercial™

For more information, visit: **www.MarketingForSolos.com/products**

2. For the "Do-It-With-Help-And-Coaching" Type of Solo ...

If you're a do-it-yourself type of solo, but also like a little help, coaching and guidance along the way, Jeanna has the perfect solution: her interactive workshops, seminars and bootcamps! As as participant Jeanna will come along beside you, to coach and mentor you every step of the way. So you'll not only learn what works for marketing your services successfully, but you'll also have the personal guidance of *the* expert on marketing a one-person small business.

Jeanna offers interactive workshops, seminars and bootcamps on the following subjects ...

- Comprehensive, Workhorse Website™
- Marketing Mentoring Groups
- Niche Marketing
- Online Marketing
- Search Engine Optimization
- Social Media Marketing
- Video Marketing
- What Do You Do? Commercial™

For more information, visit: **www.MarketingForSolos.com/coaching**

3. For the "Done-for-You" Type of Solo ...

And finally if you're the type of solo small business owner who wants to hire someone else to do all of your marketing for you, then Jeanna's comprehensive "done-for-you" services may be just what you've been looking for.

Jeanna offers the following "done-for-you" services ...

- Brochure and Collateral Materials Design, Copywriting and Development
- Comprehensive, Workhorse Website™ Design and Development
- Direct Mail Design, Copywriting, Coordination and Fulfillment
- Online Marketing Development and Implementation
- Search Engine Optimization Services
- Video Marketing Development and Implementation

For more information, visit: **www.MarketingForSolos.com/services**

Recommended Resources (From Other Vendors)

*Resources Jeanna uses for her solo small business and/or for her clients businesses are marked with an asterisk. Jeanna recommends these resources from personal experience with them; however, no guarantees are made or implied. It is highly recommended that you do your own research. Other resources are listed for your convience, and this is by no means an exhaustive list. Jeanna accepts no responsibility or liability of any kind for the product, service or results you receive (or don't receive) from using any of these resources.

Article Marketing Directories
*Ezine Articles   www.ezinearticles.com
The biggest and the best free article submission directory as far as traffic and visitors. This is a great website to post the articles you write to market your solo small business.

Distribute Your Articles   www.distributeyourarticles.com

This is another great website and service to distribute the articles you write to market your solo small business, however unlike Ezine Articles there is a fee to use there services.

Client Gifts

*Fairytale Brownies   www.brownies.com

These are fantastic brownies! I always get a lot of thank you notes, emails and calls from my clients when I send them these yummies.

*Wine Country Gift Baskets   www.winecountrygiftbaskets.com

By far the best and most affordable gift baskets anywhere (in my humble opinion). Baskets that cost $50 here, would cost hundreds elsewhere. These make awesome client gifts.

*Starbucks Corporate Gifts   www.starbuckscardb2b.com

You can order Starbucks cards in bulk, pre-attached to a card carrier with your personal message...such as "Thank you for your business, XYZ Design Company." A minimum order of 15 cards is required and you can order in any denomination from $5 upward.

*Omaha Steaks   www.omahasteaks.com

Holy cow these steaks rock! If you really want to thank a client the right way, you really cannot go wrong with Omaha Steaks. Everytime I send these to clients, I get calls thanking me profusely!

eZine Software

*Aweber   www.aweber.com

I use Aweber to manage my email and eZine lists, and I love it. I think it is the easiest and best solution on the market. I highly recommend that you check out Aweber.

*Constant Contact   www.constantcontact.com

I also use Constant Contact for HTML graphically based eZines.

*iContact   www.icontact.com

Visit http://MarketingForSolos.iContact.com (without www at the front) and enter coupon code: SUCCESS to receive $10 off their services.

Mailing Lists

*InfoUSA   www.infousa.com

I use InfoUSA for many of my clients, as well as, my own direct mail campaigns. InfoUSA has very reasonable prices and a lot of different lists, such as household consumers, corporate executives, new small businesses and professionals such as lawyers, doctors and other medical personnel.

SRDS   www.srds.com

SRDS stands for Standard Rate and Data Service. You can find info on their website or you can find the books listing mailing lists and brokers at your library. The bigger and better funded the library is, the more recent edition of the SRDS books they'll have. I have not used SRDS, but I have heard good things from other colleagues.

DMA   www.the-dma.org

You can search the Direct Marketing Association's (DMA) website and find many other mailing list brokers with many different offerings at many different prices.

Press Releases
*Marc Harty   www.onlineprmadeeasy.com

Marc's teaching on online press release is one of the best on the topic. If you want to learn how to write and market your solo small business with press releases, this is the program for you.

*PR Web   www.prweb.com

PR Web is an online press release distribution service that will get your release distributed to many online news sites and found in the search engines. It's widely considered the best service available.

Referral & Leads Groups
*BNI   www.bni.com

Business Network International (BNI) is, in my opinion, hands down, the very best referral organization you can join. It is not a leads group, but a word-of-mouth referral organization. I recommend that all solo small business owners seriously consider joining BNI.

Chambers of Commerce

Many Chambers of Commerce have leads groups, as well as, provide great networking opportunities. There are way too many chambers to list here. Check your local phone book or Yellow Pages or Google "Chambers of Commerce" and your city to find more information.

Social Media
*Ingrid Elfver   www.socialmediaforsolos.com

My good friend Ingrid Elfver is one of the very best teachers on social media strategies that actually work to make money and attract clients. She is also an expert in teaching people how to automate many social media tasks so you don't spend all of your time doing social media.

Amazon   www.amazon.com

Search Amazon for "social media" and you'll find a ton of titles (some good, some not so good). Two books I recommend are *Twitter Power* by Joel Comm and *Facebook Marketing: An Hour a Day* by Chris Treadaway and Mari Smith

Speaking & Conducting Seminars

*Fred Gleeck www.fredgleeck.com

I have learned a lot from Fred Gleeck. He has many books, products and information on speaking and conducting seminars, as well as, many other topics.

*Speak and Grow Rich www.speakandgrowrich.com

Dottie Walters is the Author of *Speak and Grow Rich*, which is the classic book on speaking.

James Malinchak www.bigmoneyspeaker.com

James has several programs and bootcamps teaching individuals and small business owners how to become a speaker and get paid speaking gigs. One of his specialities is teaching people how to speak to the college market.

Toastmasters International www.toastmasters.org

Toastmasters is a great organization that can help you improve you speaking, presentation and communication skills.

Amazon www.amazon.com

Search Amazon for "speaking and seminars" and you will find a plethora of books available. One I recommend is *Getting Started in Speaking, Training, or Seminar Consulting* by Bob Bly.

Surveys

Survey Monkey www.surveymonkey.com
Zoomerang www.zoomerang.com

Teleseminars & Webinars

Free Conference Call www.freeconferencecall.com
GoTo Meeting www.gotomeeting.com

Web Hosting

*HostGator www.hostgator.com

I use HostGator for almost all of my website hosting needs and for my clients as well. They have great customer support, service and prices. And are truly one of the best in the business and I highly recommend them!

*BlueHost www.bluehost.com

Another great hosting company I use and recommend.

Web Statistics

Google Analytics www.google.com/analytics/
Get Clicky www.getclicky.com

For links to other recommended resources, please visit:

www.MarketingForSolos.com

Index